The PrairiErth Farm CookBook

Katie Bishop

ISBN: 1484850637
ISBN-13: 9781484850633

GRATITUDE

I want to send a special shout-out to a few folks:

First... My 2011 CSA members. You guys are so awesome. You helped grow our farm into what it is today. You sent me tasty recipes, useful preserving tips, TONS of encouragement and a constant smiling face. Your patience and trust kept us going. Thank you for making our first CSA experience a great one!

To my family for putting up with my constant rambling about farming and for all your unrelenting love and support.

To my father-in-law Dave, without your foresight, wealth of knowledge, and the generous tendency to share it, plus a huge dose of patience none of this would be possible.

Hans... thanks for leading us toward our dreams. You've sacrificed so much to provide safe and healthy food for our community. You're my hero and I love you!

TABLE OF CONTENTS

I wasn't always a farmer and <u>definitely</u> wasn't always a whiz in the kitchen. Before I met my husband Hans I liked to stay out late, sleep in until noon and usually my breakfast, lunch and dinner involved take-out or a pre-packaged frozen meal. I thought I was healthy by eating low fat, low calorie, sugar free "food." I had no idea how to cook meat, or anything else for that matter, beyond boiling water for pasta. The microwave was my friend. I think you're getting the point.

But then this guy walked into my life. Both discontent with our office jobs, we knew we needed something a little more meaningful in our lives. We started growing vegetables on his Dad's 300 acre organic farm. I'd always had a green thumb and knew that organic was the only way to nourish our planet (not that I ate in a way that exemplified my beliefs). I also had a little hippy streak in me and thought it would be "cool" to be an organic farmer. I imagined laying under a tree, listening to the Grateful Dead, growing flowers and wearing clothes made out of hemp. It only took about 2 hours of actual farm work to make me realize there is very little lounging (but I do manage to squeeze in some Dead now and again).

Ultimately farming not only brought me closer to my food but also closer to the kitchen. I had to deal with new vegetables I had never eaten, let alone cooked with. My counters were full of surplus or "seconds" (ever been faced with the challenge of utilizing 3 bushel baskets full of green beans?). I wasn't prepared for any of it. I didn't know what it meant to roast. Or sauté. Or blanch. I didn't have sharp knives. Or a garlic press. Or a food processor. I had to learn how to can. And dry. And freeze.

Overwhelming? Yes. Totally fun and exciting? Absolutely! I refused to look at this whole experience as anything other than the opportunity to ROCK in the kitchen! I don't want you to be intimidated by good food. So here's my chance to help!

For more information visit us at: www.PrairiErthFarm.com

You've got all this fresh food.

Now what?

I suppose the biggest challenge people face in the kitchen is not having quick, exciting and easy ways to prepare their fresh produce. The next challenge is what to do with the surplus you get either from your CSA share, the market or your own garden. I have the same difficulties too. So this cookbook is part cooking inspiration, part vegetable 411 and part path to "putting up" your extras! It's arranged by vegetable type. I find it easiest to locate a recipe based on the ingredient I have, not the type of meal I'm preparing.

First, the recipes: These are some of my personal concoctions, along with family and customer favorites and my versions of interesting dishes I've discovered perusing the glossy pages of Gourmet magazine, the old black and white episodes of Julia Child and the countless Barefoot Contessa cookbooks I proudly display in my bookcase. I may not be a trained chef but I am resourceful!

The vegetable 411 is just interesting tidbits about either how we grow those veggies or what types of awesome super powers they possess! It's a bird, it's a plane. It's a rutabaga! (sorry... they don't wear capes!)

I think one of the best parts of this book is the "putting up" part. Here in the Midwest it's hard to eat local vegetables year round because we can't always GROW them year round. Preserving your surplus allows you to eat local and organic throughout all four seasons. Trust me, you'll thank us in February when you have pasta with fresh heirloom tomato sauce!

A

Arugula

Great in salads or topped on pizzas, tossed in pastas or soups! Arugula, like other greens, is rich in many essential vitamins and minerals. It's an excellent source of antioxidants and is also known to fight the occurrence of cancers such as colon, breast and prostate. Yeah, yeah, yeah.... but they taste good too! If arugula is too peppery or spicy for you try cooking it rather than eating it raw. Throwing it in soup or sautéing it will mellow out the flavor.

Storing Arugula: Wrap a damp towel around your arugula and store in a plastic bag in the refrigerator.

Preserving Arugula: You can freeze arugula for later use much like other greens. Clean well, blanch in boiling water for 2 minutes and then quickly submerge in ice water to stop the cooking process. Drain and pack into freezer bags, making sure to squish all the air out. Lay flat in the freezer and you'll have arugula all year long to add to soups, casseroles, omelets, etc.

Arugula and Fennel Salad

Ingredients:

2 fennel bulbs

2 cups arugula

1 lemon, juiced

Parmesan cheese

Extra virgin olive oil

Ground pepper

Directions: Loosely arrange the arugula on the bottom of a salad bowl, then add some ground pepper and drizzle some olive oil on top.

Cut off the stems and leafy tops of the fennel, then finely slice the fennel into thin rounds and spread the slices over the arugula. Pour the lemon juice over the fennel and arugula then drizzle with more olive oil and grind more pepper on top.

Shave the parmesan and cover the salad with the cheese, then serve.

Arugula, Caramelized Onion and Goat Cheese Pizza

Ingredients:

1 Tablespoon olive oil

1 red onion, sliced

3 cups arugula, washed, dried and coarsely chopped

Salt

Ground black pepper

4 whole-wheat tortillas, 6-inches-ish in diameter

2 ounces goat cheese (local favorite is Prairie Fruits Goat Cheese! Yum!)

Directions: Preheat the oven to 400 degrees. Put the oil and onions in a medium skillet and cook over very low heat, stirring occasionally, until onions are soft and caramelized, about 15 minutes. Turn the heat up to medium and add the arugula. Cook until the arugula is wilted, about 1 minute. Season with salt and pepper. Place the tortillas on a baking sheet and top each with some of the arugula/ onion mixture. Crumble some goat cheese on top of each, and bake for 10 minutes. Allow to cool for a few minutes and cut each pizza into 4 triangles.

Arugula Pesto
Ingredients:
4 cups (packed) arugula leaves
1/4 cup pine nuts, toasted (pine nuts can be pricey, so I use walnuts & it tastes great!)
1/4 cup freshly grated Parmesan cheese
1/4 cup olive oil
Salt and pepper

Directions: Prepare an ice water bath in a large bowl, and bring a large pot of water to a boil. Immediately immerse all the arugula and stir so that it blanches evenly. Blanch for about 15 seconds. Remove, shake off the excess water, then plunge the arugula into the ice water bath and stir again so it cools as fast as possible. Drain well. This is an important step, otherwise the pesto can taste bitter.

Blend drained arugula, nuts and Parmesan cheese, salt and pepper in processor until almost smooth. With machine running, gradually add olive oil; process until well blended. Season pesto to taste with salt and pepper. (Can be made ahead. Cover and let stand up to 2 hours at room temperature or refrigerate up to 1 day. Bring to room temperature before using.)

This pesto can be frozen too, spoon into an ice cube tray and freeze individual portions! Once frozen, just pop out the cubes and store in a freezer bag. If you're making soups, sauces, or stir-fries just throw a cube or two in!

Lemon Fusilli with Arugula

Ingredients:

1 Tablespoon good olive oil

1 Tablespoon minced garlic (2 cloves)

2 cups heavy cream

3 lemons

salt and ground black pepper

1 bunch broccoli

1 pound dried fusilli pasta

1/2 pound baby arugula (or 2 bunches of common arugula, leaves roughly chopped)

1/2 cup freshly grated Parmesan

1 pint grape or cherry tomatoes, halved

Directions: Heat the olive oil in a medium saucepan over medium heat, add the garlic, and cook for 60 seconds. Add the cream, the zest from 2 lemons, the juice of 2 lemons, 2 teaspoons of salt, and 1 teaspoon of pepper. Bring to a boil, then lower the heat and simmer for 15 to 20 minutes, until it starts to thicken. Meanwhile, cut the broccoli in florets and discard the stem. Cook the florets in a pot of boiling salted water for 3 to 5 minutes, until tender but still firm. Drain the broccoli and run under cold water to stop the cooking. Set aside. Bring a large pot of water to a boil, add 1 tablespoon of salt and the pasta, and cook according to the directions on the package, about 12 minutes, stirring occasionally. Drain the pasta in a colander and place it back into the pot. Immediately add the cream mixture and cook it over medium-low heat for 3 minutes, until most of the sauce has been absorbed in the pasta. Pour the hot pasta into a large bowl, add the arugula, Parmesan, tomatoes, and cooked broccoli. Cut the last lemon in half lengthwise, slice it 1/4-inch thick crosswise, and add it to the pasta. Toss well, season to taste, and serve hot.

Arugula and Pear Salad

Ingredients:

1/2 cup walnut halves

5 to 6 cups arugula, cleaned and dried

1 Bosc or Anjou pear, thinly sliced

1 lemon

3 tablespoons extra-virgin olive oil, eyeball it

Salt and freshly ground black pepper

8 ounces Gorgonzola or blue cheese crumbles

Directions: Toast nuts in small pan over medium heat until fragrant. Cool. Combine arugula and pear in a salad bowl, add nuts then dress the salad with lemon juice and olive oil, salt and pepper. Top salad with lots of blue cheese crumbles.

B

Basil

Ahhh... there's nothing better than a tomato, mozz and basil sandwich is there? I think it's probably one of the most loved and used herbs in the entire US of A. We've grown many varieties but still rely on just a few due to their reliability and wonderful flavor. Basil is easy to grow and a pleasure to work around since it's smell is so invigorating. If you have the opportunity try some of the different varieties like lemon basil (try putting some freshly picked leaves in your lemonade!) or thai basil (great in stir-fries!).

Storing basil: Basil is quite happy with its stems in a glass of water, out of the way of sunlight or direct heat (top of the stove.... not a good idea!). If you want to store it in the refrigerator, wrap it in a damp cloth and store it in the door (which is the warmest part). Basil leaves will turn black if the temperature is too low.

Preserving basil: You can very easily dry basil for future use by rubber banding a bunch of basil in a warm, well ventilated area for a few days. Store in an air tight container until your ready to use it. You can also lightly chop or rip up leaves. Place pieces in an ice cube tray and add enough water just to cover. Freeze and once frozen pop out the cubes, place in a freezer-safe container and save for sauces or soups. This will actually work with many different types of herbs. I like to freeze mint for lemonade or ice tea. Or freeze rosemary in chicken broth. Just keep in mind that you will lose some flavor when freezing fresh herbs. Another option for basil (or even cilantro) is pesto! I love, love, love pesto! Here's how:

Rockin' Pesto

Honestly, this isn't really MY pesto recipe. Pesto is pesto... there are many variations. But this is the recipe I use. It makes a lot of pesto, because I like to freeze my leftovers. Nothing like a garden pesto in the dead of winter. You can freeze pesto in ice cube trays for individual servings. Just pop out the frozen cubes and store in the freezer until you're ready to use them!

Ingredients:
1 cup walnuts or pine nuts
salt and ground pepper
8 cups lightly packed fresh basil leaves
3 garlic cloves
2/3 cup extra-virgin olive oil

Directions: Preheat oven to 350 degrees. Spread nuts on a baking sheet; toast 8 to 10 minutes. Let cool completely. In a food processor, combine nuts, basil, and garlic; season generously with salt and pepper. Process until nuts are finely chopped. With machine running, pour oil in a steady stream through the feed tube; process until smooth. Use immediately, or freeze.

Blackberry-Basil Crisp

Basil is wonderful in desserts. Don't run away from mixing savory herbs into your sweet treats.

Ingredients:
6 cups of blackberries
8 fresh basil leaves, cut into thin ribbons
Juice of half a lemon
2 cups of rolled oats (not the instant variety)
¾ cups of ground flaxseed
1/3 cup butter, melted
½ cup of brown sugar
pinch of salt

Directions: Preheat oven to 350 degrees. Mix together blackberries, lemon juice, basil, and salt in a 9X9 baking dish. In a bowl, combine oats, flaxseed, sugar and melted butter. Mix until it's crumbly and sprinkle on top of berry and basil mixture. Place the baking pan on a cookie sheet and bake in the oven for 25-30 minutes until the top is golden brown and crisp and the fruit is bubbling. You could poor some heavy cream over the top or freshly whipped cream or even a scoop of vanilla ice cream!

Lemon Basil Chicken Salad
Ingredients:
4 cups of cooked, diced chicken
1 stalk of celery, finely diced
½ cup of fresh basil leaves, chopped
½ cup of finely chopped nuts (walnuts, pecans, almonds)
½ cup of sour cream
½ cup of mayonnaise
1 ½ teaspoons of fresh lemon juice
Salt and pepper

Directions: Combine chicken, celery, basil and nuts. Set aside. In another bowl combine sour cream, lemon, salt and pepper. Add to chicken and gently coat. Best served chilled and tasted even better if made the night before.

Basil Peach Sangria
Basil goes good with fruit. Fruit goes good with wine. Wine goes good with lots of things.
Ingredients:
¾ cup of white sugar or ½ cup of agave nectar
1 cup of loosely packed fresh basil leaves
3 cups of sliced, ripe peaches
¼ cup of fresh lemon juice
1 bottle of white wine (I prefer Pinot Grigio for this)

Directions: Peel and pit your peaches. Put them in a food processor or blender on medium and pulse until they become a thick pulp.

In a saucepan, combine sugar, basil leaves, lemon juice and half of the pulp. Bring to a simmer. Crush the basil leaves with the back of a wooden spoon to release their flavor. Simmer until sugar is just melted. Remove from heat and let cool.

Strain the basil mixture into a picture filled with ice cubes. Pour in the bottle of wine and remaining peach pulp. Stir and serve!

Beans

If you've never grown green beans then you'd never know the labor that is involved in harvesting these luscious pods of delight. I wish Hans and I had young children of our own so that we could make that their primary chore. It's a lot of bending over or crouching. Not my favorite thing to do. However, what I do love about green beans is snapping them. I feel transported to another era. Sitting on the front porch, a big bowel in my lap brimming with green beans and another bowl at my feet catching the snapped beans. Grab a green bean. Snap. Drop them in the bucket. A rhythm starts to develop as I stare off into the fields daydreaming about what yummy dishes I'm going to make. The epitome of summer!

Storing Green Beans: Store unwashed beans in a bag kept in the refrigerator crisper drawer. Whole beans stored this way should keep for about seven days.

Preserving Green Beans: There's a couple of delicious ways to put back green beans. You can either a) blanch and freeze them or b) Can them! Freezing is super easy, just wash them really well, remove the tough stems, blanch them for a couple minutes, immerse them in ice water, drain and pack into freezer bags.

With canning there are many different recipes out there. I'll share my dilly bean recipe but I encourage you to search around the web, ask neighbors or get the Ball Blue Book. It's full of excellent canning recipes and all the instructions you need for canning. You can usually find it near the canning supplies, in the magazine section at the grocery store or at a book store.

Canned Dilly Beans

Ingredients:

2 lbs. trimmed green beans (1/2 a pound for each jar)

4 heads dill (not the frilly dill leaves... the flower heads)

4 cloves garlic

2-1/2 cups vinegar

2-1/2 cups water

1/4 cup canning salt (don't substitute regular salt, this is chemistry!)

Directions: Pack beans lengthwise into hot jars, leaving 1/4 inch head space. To each pint add 1 clove garlic and 1 head dill. Combine remaining ingredients in a large sauce pot (non-reactive, like an enamel or glass pot). Bring to a boil. Pour hot liquid over beans, leaving 1/4 inch head space. Remove air bubbles. Adjust caps. Process pints and quarts 10 minutes in boiling water bath. Yield: about 4 pints.

Green Bean Salad with Pickled Onions

Ingredients:

1 pound green beans

1/2 a fennel bulb (about 1/2 pound)

1 stalk celery

1/2 medium red onion

1 Tablespoon lemon juice

1/4 cup red wine vinegar

1/4 cup water

1 Tablespoon salt

1 1/2 teaspoons sugar

2 Tablespoons plus 2 teaspoons olive oil

Directions: If you've got an adjustable blade slider (aka Mandolin), time to make it earn its keep! Very thinly slice half your fennel bulb, your celery and your half onion. If you don't have a fancy slicer, just slice them thinly with a knife. Toss the fennel with lemon juice to prevent browning and also because it makes it extra delicious.

In a small bowl, whisk together the vinegar, water, salt and sugar together. Add the onions and set them aside for about an hour. If you don't have an hour, 30 minutes will still pickle them to deliciousness but they will only get better with age.

Meanwhile, bring a large pot of salted water to boil. Trim off the tough stems and snap in two pieces. Boil beans until crisp-tender, about 4 to 5 minutes for regular green beans. Plunge in an ice water bath. Drain and pat dry. (If you have no patience for the precision of ice water baths, take the green beans out a full minute early as they will continue cooking as they cool.)

Assemble your salad: Toss green beans with most of fennel, all of celery and half of the pickled red onions. Sprinkle two tablespoons of the red onion pickling liquid and two tablespoons of olive oil over the mixture. Season generously with salt and pepper. Taste, adjust seasonings and ingredient levels to your preferences — we found we wanted more fennel, red onion and pickling liquid.

Sautéed Green Beans with Herb Butter
Ingredients:
1 Tablespoon butter, softened
3 medium garlic cloves, minced
1 teaspoon chopped fresh thyme leaves
1 teaspoon olive oil
1 Lb green beans , tough stems cut off , beans snapped in two
Salt & pepper
2 teaspoons fresh lemon juice 1
Tablespoon chopped fresh parsley (optional)

Directions: In a small bowl, combine butter, garlic, and thyme; set aside. In a 12 inch skillet, heat olive oil over medium heat until it's just smoking. Add beans plus 1/4 teaspoon salt and 1/8 teaspoon black pepper; cook and stir for 8-10 minutes.

Stir in herb butter and cook beans for 1-3 minutes longer, or until beans are crisp-tender. Toss with lemon juice and parsley if desired; serve immediately.

Spicy Grilled Green Beans
Ingredients:
1 pound of fresh green beans (about three huge fistfuls)
1 Tablespoon of olive oil
Pinch of cumin
Pinch of coriander
½ teaspoon of smoked, hot paprika
salt and pepper to taste

Directions: Snap off tips and stems of green beans. Wash well and pat dry. Put them in a large bowl and drizzle olive oil over the top. Toss well to coat. In a small bowl mix cumin, coriander and paprika. Sprinkle over the beans and add salt and pepper to taste.

Heat grill to low (if using charcoal, cook beans around the outside of the hot coals). Place beans across the grates (so they don't fall in) or use a veggie grilling basket. Put lid on grill and cook for about 10 minutes until crisp. Turning throughout to make sure they cook evenly. Consider dipping into a Greek raita sauce (See cucumber recipe section for the sauce recipe!)

Beets

If there's one thing I know it's beets. Not because I particularly enjoy them because truthfully I do not. But Hans LOVES beets. He insists on eating beets almost every day they are in season so I've become quite familiar with beets. I'm blessed that he loves beets so much because they are SO good for him. They have been shown to be an immunity booster, guard against cancer and heart disease.

Beets contain magnesium, calcium, iron and phosphorus! They are also considered a high fiber food and contain vitamins A and C as well as niacin! You can't beat that! Seriously... beets are a SUPER FOOD! If that weren't enough beet tops are incredibly good for you too! We grow golden beets, a variety called Chioggia that are candy-cane striped on the inside, an heirloom variety called Detroit Dark Red and many others! If regular red beets don't tickle your fancy try a different variety. Some have a less earthy taste, some are more sweet. Maybe you'll find one that suits you.

Storing Beets: Cut the majority of the greens and their stems from the beet roots, so they do not pull away moisture away from the root. Leave about two inches of the stem attached to prevent the roots from "bleeding." Do not wash beets before storing. Place in a plastic bag and wrap the bag tightly around the beets, squeezing out as much of the air from the bag as possible, and place in refrigerator where they will keep for up to 3 weeks.

Store the unwashed greens in a separate plastic bag squeezing out as much of the air as possible. Place in refrigerator where they will keep fresh for about four days.

Preserving Beets: Pickling beets is really easy and a wonderful way to dive into the fun of canning because pickling beets very simple and isn't time consuming. Go to www.freshpreserving.com for free access to lots of Ball's canning recipes; including a phenomenal pickled beet recipe! You can freeze the leafy tops by blanching for 2 minutes in boiling water, then immediately emerging the tops in ice water. Drain, pack into quart size freezer bags and squish all the air out. Lay flat in the freezer and you can throw these greens in any soup, casserole, egg dish or dip.

Rosemary Roasted Beets

Ingredients:

5 large beets, tops removed (reserve for another meal!)

4 small sprigs fresh rosemary, minced

2-3 cloves garlic, sliced thin

1-2 Tablespoons of olive oil

Salt & pepper

Directions: Preheat your oven to 400°F. Peel the beets. I do this in the sink, with water running slightly. This helps to keep staining of your hands and cutting boards to a minimum. You could also fill the sink and do it under the water. Some people leave the skins on. Cut beets into wedges (each beet should make 8 wedges). In a large bowl, add beet wedges, minced rosemary and sliced garlic. Grind in some fresh salt and pepper and toss to coat. Place in a shallow baking dish and cover. Bake in preheated oven for 30 minutes. Uncover and bake for another 30 minutes. Remove from oven and let stand for a few minutes before serving.

Beet Hummus

CSA Member Megan Owens

Ingredients:

one very large beet (or two medium beets)

2 Tablespoons of tahini

2 cups chickpeas

2 medium cloves of garlic

1 small lemon

Directions: Peel and chop beets into medium cubes, put into sauce pan with just enough water to cover beets and simmer until beets can be easily pierced with a fork, then drain the water. Combine beets, chickpeas, garlic, lemon juice, salt and tahini in food processor and blend. Add a little water if the consistency is too thick for your liking.

Beet Walnut Dip

CSA member Amy Tell

This recipe was given to me from a 2011 CSA member and she swore I'd like it. (She knew of my distaste for beets). Surprisingly, it was really tasty! So if you're not sure you'll like beets, this is a good place to start! Thanks Amy!

Ingredients

1 pound beets (4 smallish beets), scrubbed

1 cup walnuts

1 clove garlic, smashed and peeled

3 teaspoons sherry vinegar or lemon juice

a few fresh herb leaves, such as marjoram or thyme (optional)

1 1/2 teaspoons kosher salt (or half as much table salt)

1/3 cup olive oil

1/3 cup Greek yogurt

Directions: In a small pot of water, covered, over high heat, bring the beets to a boil, then turn the heat down and simmer them until they're tender, 20-45 minutes, depending on their size. I stick a tiny knife in and call them done when I feel no resistance. Drain the beets in a colander, run cold water over them, then peel their skins and remove the stems.

Meanwhile, toast the walnuts at 350°F for five or so minutes until they smell toasty. Let them cool.

In a food processor fitted with the metal blade, whirl together the beets, walnuts, garlic, sherry vinegar or lemon juice, optional herbs, and salt, stopping to scrape down the side of the bowl every now and then, until the mixture looks like a coarse puree.

With the motor running, slowly drizzle in the olive oil, then whirl in the yogurt. Taste the mixture for salt and tang, adding more salt or vinegar/juice as needed, then scoop in a bowl and serve with crackers, veggies, or pita chips.

Chocolate Beet Cupcakes

Still can't get your kids to eat beets? Or maybe you're like me... and you just can't imagine why on earth ANYONE wants to eat these things? Well try this cake and relish in the fact that not only does it taste good, its a great way to get all the nutrients but still have your cake too!

Ingredients:

2 sticks butter, softened (bring to room temperature)

¾ cup sugar

1 ½ cups plain flour

2½ teaspoons of baking powder

½ teaspoons of salt

4 tbs Dutch process cocoa powder

4 eggs

1 cup puréed, cooked, peeled beets *

Directions: Preheat the oven to 350°. Place 12 paper baking cups in muffin pans. Combine all the ingredients, except the beets, in a large bowl and beat with an electric mixer until smooth, about 2 to 3 minutes. Then when just combined – that means you can't see any of the flour - fold in the beets.

Spoon the batter into the cups. Bake for 20 minutes. To see if cooked insert a toothpick into one and if it comes out dry they are done. Remove pan from the oven and cool for five minutes. Then remove the cupcakes and cool on a rack. Sprinkle with confectioners' sugar.

* Boil the beets in a small pot of water, covered over medium heat until tender. Depends on their size... usually 20-35 minutes. Just pierce with a fork until there's no resistance. Then slip the peels off, remove the stem and puree!

Broccoli

I love broccoli. In all shapes and forms. It's packed full of
nutrients and feel-full fiber and when you buy it fresh the
taste is so amazing there's no reason to smother it with
cheese sauce. What I don't like are the worms that also like
broccoli (hey I don't like to share!). That's part of the
challenge of organic farming I guess, but they are bright
green little guys called cabbage worms that sometimes
surprise me when I'm chopping up a bunch of that
wonderful broccoli goodness! (Actually I start screaming
and run into the other room!). Just pick the little guy off
and throw him outside. He'll appreciate it! Here's a taste
tip: So much of the wonderful broccoli flavor comes from
the stem! Don't throw that puppy away! Once you peel the
tough outer skin you can sauté, roast, steam, etc!

Storing Broccoli: Store broccoli unwashed in the
refrigerator but wrapped in a damp towel. If bought fresh,
it should last for up to 10 days.

Preserving Broccoli: Peel the leaves from the stalk. Place
broccoli in boiling water for 1 ½ minutes. Remove from hot
water and immediately submerge in an ice water bath,
then drain. Place the broccoli in a sealed plastic bag.
Broccoli can be stored in the freezer for up to 10 months.
This is an excellent way to store broccoli until you want to
enjoy broccoli cheese soup or a casserole in the winter.

Garden Pasta with Broccoli and Herbs

Need a quick dinner... this is super fast!

Ingredients:

1/2 cup (1 stick) unsalted butter, room temperature

2 Tablespoons chopped fresh basil

2 Tablespoons chopped fresh parsley

1 garlic clove, minced

2 teaspoons olive oil

8 ounces pasta (any type is fine)

2 cups small broccoli florets

1 cup of sliced cherry tomatoes

¼ teaspoon of red pepper flakes

Salt and pepper to taste

Grated Parmesan cheese

Directions: Combine the first 4 ingredients in a bowl and set aside.

Bring a pot of salted water to boil. Add olive oil. Add pasta and cook until just under al dente. Add broccoli and boil until pasta is tender, about 2 minutes longer. Drain pasta and broccoli; transfer to large serving bowl.

Add herb butter and toss well to coat. Sprinkle with red pepper flakes, salt and pepper (to taste). Gently stir in tomatoes and finally a sprinkle of parmesan cheese.

Hans' Favorite Broccoli Salad

Simple. Tasty.

Ingredients:

2 bunches broccoli, florets only (5 to 6 cups florets)

1 medium red onion, chopped

1/2 cup raisins

10 to 12 slices bacon, fried and crumbled

Dressing:

1 cup mayonnaise

2 Tablespoons balsamic vinegar

2 teaspoons sugar

Salt and pepper to taste

Directions: Separate florets from broccoli stalks. Save the remainder of the broccoli for another use or freeze for later. Combine salad ingredients; top with dressing mixture. Chill and serve. That's as easy as it gets!

Oven Roasted Broccoli with Parmesan, Garlic & Lemon

Ingredients:

1 1/2 lbs Broccoli, cut into bite sized florets.

Olive Oil

4 cloves garlic, minced

Zest of 1/2 a lemon

1/2 cup freshly grated Parmesan

Salt and Pepper

Directions: Preheat the oven to 450F. In a large bowl, add the broccoli florets, drizzle liberally with olive oil and toss to coat. Add the lemon zest and garlic, and toss again until well mixed. Spread the broccoli on a large baking sheet in a single layer and roast in the oven for 10 minutes. Sprinkle with Parmesan and return to the oven until the Parmesan begins to bubble and the broccoli is tender and golden around the edges, about another 10 minutes. Sprinkle with salt and pepper and squeeze a wedge or two of lemon over right before serving.

Winter Veggie Slaw

Ingredients:
One head of broccoli
10 brussel sprouts
2 stalks of celery
1 smallish head of nappa cabbage (you can use regular but
I like the flavor of nappa better)
3 carrots
Dressing:
½ cup of mayo
1 Tablespoon of good mustard
2 Tablespoons of rice wine or champagne vinegar
Pinch of red pepper flakes
salt and pepper

Directions: Shred cabbage and carrots in a food processor
or slice thinly. Peel tough outer skin from stalks of broccoli
and slice them in half lengthwise. Finely dice into about ½
inch cubes. Cut up the head of the broccoli into small
florets. Peel any browned or tough outer leaves from the
brussel sprouts and finely slice those as well. (Perfect
slivers of veggies isn't necessary. This is a slaw after all)
Slice celery in half lengthwise and dice about the same size
as the broccoli stalks. Combine all your veggies in a nice big
bowl.

To make the dressing mix the mayo, mustard, and vinegar.
Add a pinch of red pepper flakes (or more if you dare)
along with a sprinkle of salt and pepper to taste. Add the
dressing to your big bowl of veggies and mix well. Taste
and add more salt and pepper. This dish is great served
immediately after making but is fantastic if refrigerated
overnight too.

Vegan Cream of Broccoli Soup

Ingredients:

1 Tablespoon olive oil
2 cloves of garlic, chopped
1/4 cup diced yellow onion
1 Tablespoon of peeled, finely chopped ginger
5 cups broccoli, chopped (use those stems but peel them first!)
3 cups of peeled diced potatoes
Water, as needed
Salt and pepper, to taste
1 smallish bunch of fresh parsley, roughly chopped
1 cup coconut milk, or to taste

Directions: Heat the olive oil in a large soup pot or dutch oven set over medium heat and stir in the garlic, onion, ginger. Add in the cut up broccoli and gold potatoes. Add *just* enough water to cover the vegetables- not too much. You can always thin the soup later, if you need to.

Add the chopped parsley. Season with sea salt and fresh pepper, to taste.

Bring the vegetables to a high simmer. Cover the pot, and reduce the heat to a medium simmer. Cook for twenty minutes or so, until the potatoes are fork tender.

Remove the pot from the heat. Use an immersion blender to puree the soup.

Return the pot to the stove and add in the coconut milk. Stir and heat through gently but don't bring to a boil.

Taste test and adjust seasonings.

Broccoli Rabe (aka Rapini)

Also known as Rapini! Popular in almost all continents except North America. I don't get it. But it's a great vegetable that has many of the same health benefits of broccoli and cabbage. Sometimes it can taste a little bitter, but a great way to fix that problem is to boil it first before you sauté it. Works like a charm every time! Or maybe you'll like that pungent bitter taste that it's so well known for.

Storing Broccoli Rabe: Wrap in a damp towel and store in your crisper section for up to 7 days.

Pasta with Sausage & Broccoli Rabe
Ingredients:
1 pound orecchiette
1 Tablespoon olive oil
1 pound sweet Italian sausage, casings removed
2 cloves garlic, finely chopped
2 1/2 cups low-sodium chicken broth
1/8 teaspoon crushed red pepper
1 bunch broccoli rabe
4 Tablespoons butter, cut into pieces
1 cup grated Parmesan
salt and black pepper

Directions: Cook the pasta according to the package directions. Drain and return it to the pot.

Meanwhile, heat the oil in a large saucepan over medium heat. Add the sausage and cook, breaking it up with a spoon, until it's no longer pink, 5 to 6 minutes. Stir in the garlic and cook 1 minute. Add the broth and red pepper and bring to a boil. Add the broccoli rabe and simmer, covered, until tender, 3 to 4 minutes. Stir in the butter and Parmesan and cook, uncovered, until the sauce thickens slightly, 1 to 2 minutes. Toss the pasta with the sausage mixture and ¼ teaspoon each salt and pepper.

Vegetarian Pasta with Broccoli Rabe
Ingredients:
Kosher salt, to taste
1 bunch rapini, roughly chopped
1/3 cup extra-virgin olive oil
6 cloves garlic, crushed
3/4 teaspoons of crushed red chili flakes1
2 oz. orecchiette (or similar shaped pasta)
2 Tablespoons of. lemon zest
4 oz. goat cheese, softened

Directions: Bring a pot of salted water to a boil. Add rapini and boil until crisp-tender, about 4 minutes. Using a slotted spoon, transfer rapini to a large bowl of ice water; chill. Drain rapini, pat dry, and set aside. Heat oil in a large skillet over medium heat. Add garlic and cook, stirring occasionally, until golden, about 3 minutes. Add chili flakes and cook, stirring frequently, for 30 seconds. Add rapini, toss, and remove pan from heat; set aside. Meanwhile, bring a pot of salted water to a boil. Add pasta and cook until al dente, about 10 minutes. Drain pasta and transfer pasta and lemon zest to reserved skillet over high heat. Toss to combine and season with salt. Divide pasta between bowls and add a dollop of goat cheese to each.

Rapini with Fennel and Orange

Ingredients:

1 bunch of rapini, tough stems removed, leaves and stems separated and cleaned

1 small brown onion, peeled and finely diced

1 small fennel bulb, stalks removed, split across the width and cored, finely diced

2 cloves garlic, peeled and minced

Salt and fresh ground black pepper to taste

Olive oil as needed

1/3 cup orange juice

Directions: Bring a large pot of water to a boil for the rapini. Once boiling, salt the water well . Drop the rapini stems into the water and cook for one minute. Drop in the leaves, and cook 1 minute more. Taste a stem and leaf each to see if they are tender. If not, cook a little longer and taste to check. As soon as the rapini is tender, remove it from the water and drain. Rinse with cool water to prevent over-cooking. When drained, place on a cutting board and chop finely.

Heat a 10-inch skillet over medium-high heat. When the pan is hot, add enough oil to cover the pan bottom. When the oil is hot, add the onion and fennel and sauté until vegetables are soft and starting to color a little. Add the garlic to the pan and cook for 1 minute more. Add the rapini to the pan, stirring to combine the greens with the rest of the vegetables. Drizzle with some olive oil. Sauté until the vegetables are hot, then add the orange juice, tossing to get all the vegetables wet with the juice. Cook until the juice has reduced all the way and has become a little syrupy. Be sure not to burn the vegetables. Once the juice has cooked away, season with salt and pepper and serve hot.

Brussel Sprouts

When Hans told me we were growing brussel sprouts I turned up my nose and walked away. Would we be able to sell them? Would our CSA members want them? Would I have to eat them? The truth is, I've given into the sprout hating hype and excluded them from my diet for no other reason but because of their bad reputation. I think I've had them once. When I was 5 and they came in a frozen package that my mom defrosted and heated in a pan of water on the stove. (No offense Mom... but I don't remember them tasting very good). In almost 30 years I've managed to steer clear of brussel sprouts until Hans decided to grow them. I stumbled upon this recipe that promised me a flavor explosion of pure delight. They were right! These ARE tasty! They are now one of my favorites! Here's the thing... brussel sprouts can truly rock your world if they are prepared correctly. It's all in the recipe folks.

Storing brussel sprouts: You're in luck... these babies will last weeks if stored correctly! Store them in the fridge in a bowl. The outer leaves will shrivel and wilt in the open air, but the inner (and yummy!) part of the sprout will remain protected. Remove those outer leaves before cooking.

Preserving brussel sprouts: Unless you're stuck with a TON of brussel sprouts the best thing is to just store them properly in the refrigerator and they will last a REALLY long tome. However if you want to preserve them the best home preservation method for brussels sprouts is freezing. As with any vegetable, brussels sprouts will need to be blanched prior to freezing. Wash well and blanch in boiling water for 3 minutes. Remove and submerge into an ice water bath. Drain and pat dry. Pack into freezer bags and store in the freezer.

Braised Brussels Sprouts with Mustard Butter
YES! Mustard butter! It's amazing!
Ingredients:
1 pound small, firm, bright green brussels sprouts
1/2 teaspoon salt
1/2 cup water
2 Tablespoons melted unsalted butter
2 Tablespoons Dijon mustard
Salt and freshly ground black pepper

Directions: Check each head, peel off any loose or discolored leaves. Using a paring knife, cut an X through the core end of each head. Bring sprouts, water and salt to a boil in a 2-quart saucepan over medium-high heat. Lower heat, cover and simmer. Shake pan once or twice during braising to redistribute sprouts. Cook until just tender 8 to 10 minutes. Test by piercing with a knife tip. Drain well.

Melt butter in a large skillet of medium heat. Whisk in mustard until smooth. Cook , stirring constantly until smooth and creamy, about 30 seconds.

Add sprouts to skillet, coating well with the butter mixture. Season to taste with salt and pepper and serve.

Roasted Brussel Sprouts with Balsamic Vinegar

Ingredients:

Brussels Sprouts
Olive Oil
Balsamic Vinegar
Sea Salt
Pepper

Directions: Preheat oven to roast at 375°F. Peel the outer, beat-up layers of the brussels sprouts off. Trim the end, then cut brussels sprouts in half.
Toss in a bowl with enough olive oil to coat evenly, then add balsamic vinegar, salt and pepper to taste.

Lightly oil a sheet pan, then spread out brussels sprouts, cut side down. Roast in oven for 15 min., flip the sprouts to cut side up, then roast for about 10 minutes more or until gently browned.

Golden-Crusted Brussels Sprouts

Ingredients:

24 small brussels sprouts
1 Tablespoon extra-virgin olive oil, plus more for rubbing
salt and freshly ground black pepper
1/4 cup grated parmesan

Directions: Wash the brussels sprouts well. Trim the stem ends and remove any raggy outer leaves. Cut in half from stem to top and gently rub each half with olive oil, keeping it intact (or if you're short on time just toss them in a bowl with a glug of olive oil).

Heat 1 tablespoon of olive oil in your largest skillet over medium heat. Don't overheat the skillet, or the outsides of the brussels sprouts will cook too quickly. Place the brussels sprouts in the pan flat side down (single-layer), sprinkle with a couple pinches of salt, cover, and cook for roughly 5 minutes; the bottoms of the sprouts should only show a hint of browning. Cut into or taste one of the sprouts to gauge whether they're tender throughout. If not, cover and cook for a few more minutes.

Once just tender, uncover, turn up the heat, and cook until the flat sides are deep brown and caramelized. Use a metal spatula to toss them once or twice to get some browning on the rounded side. Season with more salt, a few grinds of pepper, and a dusting of grated cheese. Serve warm.

Shaved Brussels Sprouts Salad with Almonds
Ingredients:
4 cups very thinly sliced Brussels sprouts (I've used my box grater and it works great!)
 1/2 cup Parmesan cheese, shaved with a vegetable peeler
 1/4 cup roasted chopped almonds
1/4 cup of raisins
1/4 cup extra-virgin olive oil
Salt and ground black pepper
2 Tablespoons fresh lemon juice

Directions: Toss brussels sprouts, parmesan, almonds, raisins, olive oil, and a sprinkling of salt and pepper in a medium bowl. Add lemon juice; toss to coat again. Taste and adjust seasonings. Serve.

Brussel Sprouts with Bacon and Raisins

Ingredients:

1 teaspoon of olive oil

2 slices of bacon

4 cups of brussel sprouts, trimmed and halved

1/4 cup of golden raisins

1 medium onion, finely chopped

1 Tablespoon of butter

1/2 cup of chicken stock

2 Tablespoons of apple cider vinegar

salt and pepper

Directions: Heat oil in a large heavy skillet over medium heat. Add bacon and cook until crisp. Transfer bacon to paper towels to drain. Let cool and coarsely crumble. While bacon cools, add brussel sprouts to bacon drippings in the same skillet. Season with salt and pepper. Cook, stirring often until well browned in spots and starting to soften, about 5-7 minutes. Reduce heat to low and add raisins, onion, and butter. Cook, stirring often until onion is soft, about 3 minutes. Add broth and scrape the bottom on the pan with a wooden spoon to get all the brown bits up (this is where the flavor is!) Reduce heat to medium-low and simmer until broth has reduced, about 1-2 minutes. Stir in vinegar and bacon. Season with salt and pepper. Serve hot or at room temp.

C

Cabbage

For the longest time cabbage was only in my cooking repertoire when I made coleslaw (I like to say "coldslaw" and Hans likes to give me a hard time about that). But when you've got 3 "less than perfect" cabbages in your refrigerator you just can't imagine eating that much slaw. This became problematic because I hate sauerkraut and the idea of cabbage soup makes me think of the movie Willy Wonka's Chocolate Factory... and they didn't look like the enjoyed it much. So what else is left? I've included recipes for both regular green cabbage and napa cabbage.

Storing cabbage: It's best to wrap your unwashed cabbage in some type of bag and store it in the crisper drawer of your refrigerator. It can last at least a month, but if the outside leaves start to look crummy just peel those off.

Preserving cabbage: I guess the answer is sauerkraut, although I shudder to think of anyone enjoying that stinky stuff. Seriously, the most common way to preserve cabbage is through fermentation. But sauerkraut isn't the only way. There's also kimchi, a spicy Korean dish.

Homemade Sauerkraut
Ingredients:
1 head of cabbage
a carrot or two (optional)
coarse sea or rock salt
a handful of caraway seeds
a bucket with a lid
 a rolling pin or something else which can be used as a crusher/masher

Directions: Using whatever kitchen implements you have, shred the cabbage to resemble fine shreds. Grate the carrot on a coarse grater. Add a layer of cabbage, carrot, salt and caraway seeds to your bucket. Repeat the layers until your bucket is half full. Crush with the rolling pin until cabbage starts producing liquid. Repeat the layers and keep crushing.

That's pretty much the whole process. Now weigh the cabbage down (I use half a brick wrapped in a towel and placed in a large zip lock bag) until it is below the liquid line, put the lid on. Keep it out of fridge for about 24 hours to activate the fermentation process. Then stick it in the fridge. I find the sauerkraut is ready for use after about 2 months.

Red Cabbage

From Grandma Betty Micetic

This is a family recipe of mine on my father's side. My Grandfather loved it.

Ingredients:

1 small head of red cabbage

2 Tablespoons of minced garlic

1 1/2 cup thinly sliced apples

1/2 cups of water

2 Tablespoons of vinegar

2 Tablespoons of butter

1 teaspoon of salt

1/2 cups of grape jelly (the secret ingredient!)

Directions: Combine shredded cabbage with all other ingredients. Cover and cook slowly in a stockpot or dutch oven for one hour.

Pork Shoulder Braised with Napa Cabbage

Ingredients:

5 or 6 lb pork shoulder butt, on the bone

1/2 lb slab bacon, 1 to 1.5 inches thick

1/2 napa cabbage, sliced 1/4" thick

3 medium vidalia or yellow onions, chopped

2 carrots, chopped

2 celery stalks, diced

4 or 5 cloves of garlic, minced

1 1/2 teaspoon of ground fennel seed

1 teaspoon of ground coriander seed

Parsley, thyme, and 2 bay leaves, wrapped in string

salt and pepper

dry white wine

olive oil

Directions: Preheat oven to 300F. Remove the skin from pork shoulder and score the fat. Rub 1 tsp of salt and the ground spices around the pork, let it come to room temperature for 20 minutes or so. Heat a splash of olive oil in a dutch oven until very hot. Sear all sides of the pork and then remove to the side. Slice the slab bacon 1/2 inch thick and brown it in the dutch oven, then turn the heat down to medium and remove the bacon to the side as well. Saute the onions until they start to turn translucent, then add in the carrot, celery, garlic, and spices. Place the pork shoulder on top and pour in half a bottle of white wine. Bring the liquid about 1/4 up the side of the pork, adding water if needed. Scatter the slab bacon around, place the herb bunch in the pot, and scatter around the napa cabbage. Cover and cook for two hours, then flip the shoulder and cook for another 2 hours. Skim the liquid fat off the top of the braised vegetables in the pot. With a slotted spoon to drain excess liquid, plate some of braised vegetables next to the meat and serve

Cabbage and Sausage Skillet

CSA member Sarah Hull

Ingredients:

1 small head cabbage, shredded (5 cups)

4 medium potatoes, sliced

1 medium onion, sliced and separated into rings

1 teaspoon caraway seed (optional)

1 pound cooked kielbasa or other smoked sausage link,
halved lengthwise and bias-sliced into 1-inch pieces

1 cup apple juice

2 Tablespoons brown or prepared mustard

1/2 teaspoon instant beef bouillon granules

Directions: In a 12-inch skillet combine cabbage, sliced
potatoes, onion, and, if desired, caraway seed. Top with
sausage.
In a small bowl combine apple juice, mustard, and bouillon
granules. Pour over sausage mixture in skillet. Bring
mixture to boiling; reduce heat. Cover and simmer about
30 minutes or until vegetables are tender.

Braised Cabbage

Ingredients:

1/2 head of shredded cabbage

1 teaspoon salt

2 teaspoon caraway seeds

1/2 medium onion, shredded or finely sliced

1 cup water

2-3 Tablespoon lard or butter

1 Tablespoon white vinegar

1 Tablespoon sugar

Directions: Slice the cabbage into 1/4 inch and in a pan,
steam the cabbage by adding 1 cup of water of high heat
without covering. You should stir frequently. (Approx 20
minutes) – Then add butter, sugar and vinegar. Cover and

then reduce the heat to medium to medium low. Continue to cook the cabbage until the liquid evaporates. Watch cautiously so the cabbage does not burn when the liquid is gone.

Soba Noodle Stir Fry

This is a great way to use your napa cabbage and/or bok choy!

Ingredients:

6 oz (1/2 package) soba noodles

2 heads Napa cabbage, sliced thin (my cabbages were small, so if you can only find large ones you may want to stick with 1)

1 teaspoon vegetable oil

4 heads baby Bok Choy, sliced thin (again, depends on size)

1-2 carrots, shredded

4 cloves garlic, minced

1 teaspoon ginger, minced

pinch of salt and pepper

Sauce:

2 Tablespoons rice vinegar

2 Tablespoons low sodium soy sauce

2 Tablespoons peanut sauce (you can find this in the Asian section of most grocery stores)

1 Tablespoon sesame oil

1 Tablespoon sesame seeds

1 Tablespoon hot chile sauce, like Sriracha (more or less depending on how much spice you want)

Directions: Prep your vegetables and sauce first. Set aside. Heat wok. Boil water. Heat vegetable oil in wok, then carefully add garlic, ginger and sliced cabbage. Add a pinch salt and pepper. Toss cabbage around for about 2-3 minutes until cooked through. Turn off heat and set aside. Cook noodles according to directions (about 4 minutes). When noodles are done, turn on heat under wok and add noodles to vegetable mixture. Pour sauce over noodles and vegetables and carefully toss to combine. Serve noodles in bowls with shredded carrot over top. Serve with additional hot chile sauce if desired.

Carrots

We once visited a summer camp session at the local YWCA and had the kids "taste test" our carrots and the baby carrots you buy in a bag at the grocery store. Hands down the kids liked our carrots better. I'm not surprised. They are super sweet and actually taste like a carrot! Imagine that. I never get tired of hearing people at the farmers market ooh and ahh over our purple and yellow carrots! It's hard to believe but there are people out there that think the only types of carrots out there are the baby carrots in a bag at the grocery store. Yep it's true. I think we need a carrot revolution!

Storing carrots: When you get them home cut the green tops off. (These are edible!). Store in a bag in the crisper drawer of your refrigerator. They should last for weeks.

Preserving carrots: You can definitely freeze carrots. I like to slice mine into ¼ inch slices. Blanch them for 2 minutes (5 minutes if you're freezing the entire carrot whole). Drain and submerge them in ice water. Drain again, and place in freezer bags and store in the freezer. This is perfect for soups or stir fry's but you can also just reheat them on the stove too.

Katie's ADDICTING Honey Glazed Carrots

One day I was a sautéing a carrot mindlessly... staring off into space when my gaze fell on a new bottle of honey from our beekeeper Tom. The rest was history. Since then I've discovered this dish is also pretty amazing with crumbled goat cheese right before serving. We've even added sliced almonds and a sprinkle of red pepper flakes. As is, this recipe is fantastic, but you can also consider it a nice base and build upon it with lots of different flavors!

Ingredients:

1 Tablespoon of butter

1 teaspoon of olive or sesame oil

4 carrots, sliced (I leave the skins on)

A smidge of parsley

Salt to taste

1 Tablespoon of honey (Preferably raw, organic honey)

Directions: Heat skillet with sesame oil over medium heat. Add carrots and cook, stirring frequently, for 3 minutes. Add butter and honey and continue to cook for 3 more minutes. Off the heat, sprinkle salt and parsley and serve.

Carrot & Beet Latkes

I am a lover of all things pancake!

Ingredients:

2 medium beets, coarsely grated

2 medium carrots, coarsely grated

1 medium onion, coarsely grated

2 eggs, beaten

1/4 cup all-purpose flour

3 Tablespoons olive oil

salt and pepper to taste

sour cream or creme fraiche, plus chopped chives, for serving

Directions: Combine the grated vegetables in a bowl. Add the beaten eggs, stir to combine, then stir in the flour and salt and pepper to taste.

Preheat the oven to 300 degrees F, and set a cooling rack on a sheet pan. Heat 1 1/2 tablespoons olive oil in a large skillet over medium heat. When the oil is hot, scoop 1/3 cup of the latke mixture into the skillet, and flatten to 1/4 inch thick. Scoop 3 more latkes into the skillet. Cook the 4 latkes until golden brown, about 4-6 minutes per side. Remove the latkes to the cooling rack on the sheet pan, and place them in the oven to keep the latkes warm while you cook the remaining four.

Add another 1 1/2 tablespoons oil to the skillet and cook the remaining latkes. When all the latkes are done, serve them warm with a dollop of sour cream or creme fraiche and a sprinkling of chives.

Makes 8.

Moroccan Carrot Salad

Ingredients:

4 carrots, cut into wedges

1 handful, black olives

6 radishes, sliced thinly

1 clove garlic, chopped

¼ teaspoon of paprika

½ teaspoon of ground cumin, or ½ teaspoon of cumin seeds

1 pinch cayenne pepper

1 pinch cinnamon

1 teaspoon salt

1 parsley sprigs, chopped

1 fresh lemon, squeezed

¼ cup of oil, olive

Directions: Bring a pan of water to boil. Add the carrots and cook until tender and then rinse them with cold water. Drain the carrots and mix with the olives and radishes. Mix the rest of the ingredients, including the chopped parsley and garlic, to create a marinade. Pour the marinade over the carrots, olives and radishes and serve.

Thyme-Roasted Carrots

This one is super easy... if you're new to roasting vegetables, this is a great start.

Ingredients:

10-12 whole unpeeled carrots, split lengthwise

2 Tablespoons of fresh whole thyme leaves (no stems)

2-3 Tablespoons of olive oil

1 teaspoon salt

1/4 teaspoon ground black pepper

optional: balsamic vinegar, honey, fresh rosemary sprigs

Directions Preheat oven to 400 degrees F. Cover a sheet pan with aluminum foil or parchment paper. Drizzle olive oil over carrots on the sheet pan. Season with kosher salt and ground black pepper. Toss carrots until evenly coated with oil and seasonings. Arrange carrots on sheet pan. Toss fresh thyme leaves over carrots. Roast in oven for 30-35 minutes, until golden and tender.

Gluten Free Morning Glory Muffins

Ingredients:

2 cups gluten free all-purpose flour mix

1 cup white sugar

2 teaspoon of baking soda

2 teaspoon of ground cinnamon

¼ teaspoon of salt

2 cups shredded carrots

½ cup raisins

½ cup chopped walnuts

½ cup coconut

¼ cup cranberries

3 eggs

1 cup vegetable oil

2 teaspoons vanilla extract

Directions: Preheat oven to 350°f. Grease 12 muffin cups, or line with paper muffin liners. In a large bowl, mix together flour, sugar, baking soda, cinnamon, and salt. Stir in the carrot, raisins, nuts, coconut, and cranberries. In a separate bowl, beat together eggs, oil, and vanilla. Stir egg mixture into the fruit/flour mixture, just until moistened. Scoop batter into prepared muffin cups. Bake in preheated oven for 20 minutes (toothpick inserted into center of a muffin comes out clean.)

Cauliflower

It's soapbox time! I'm tired of cauliflower not getting the health praise it deserves! It's always overshadowed by broccoli and it's just not fair. Yes, broccoli is great. But did you know cauliflower is PACKED... PACKED I say... with vitamin C? Did you know that studies have shown cauliflower has been known to prevent types of cancers like breast, colon, prostate, bladder and ovarian? It has great anti-inflammation and anti-oxidant properties and the vitamin K content is through the roof. Trust me... your body is begging for cauliflower.

Storing cauliflower: The heads, when left intact, will last much longer in the fridge than if you wash it, cut it up into florets and stored in a bag. Just wrap the head loosely in a cloth or bag and store in the fridge. Should last up to two weeks.

Preserving cauliflower: I have about 1 dozen bags of it in the freezer right now. Just wash and cut into pieces. Blanch in boiling water for 3 minutes, drain and submerge into an ice water bath. Drain again and pack into freezer bags and store in the freezer.

Silky Cauliflower Soup
Adapted from David Lieberman
Ingredients:
1 head cauliflower
2 Tablespoons extra-virgin olive oil
1 small onion, chopped
2 cloves garlic, minced
1 quart low-sodium chicken stock
1/2 cup finely grated Parmesan
Salt and ground black pepper

Directions: Remove and discard the leaves and thick core. Coarsely chop head and reserve.
Heat the olive oil in a large saucepan or soup pot over medium heat and add the onion and garlic. Cook until softened, but not browned, about 5 minutes. Add the cauliflower and stock and bring to a boil. Reduce the heat to a simmer, cover, and cook until the cauliflower is very soft and falling apart, about 15 minutes. Remove from heat and, using a hand held immersion blender, puree the soup, or puree in small batches in a blender and return it to the pot. Add the Parmesan and stir until smooth. Season, to taste, with salt and black pepper. Keep warm until ready to serve.

Broccoli/Cauliflower Casserole
From CSA member Sylvia Bradley
Ingredients:
1 head cauliflower, cut up
2 heads broccoli, cut up
8 oz. mushrooms, sliced
2 small onions, chopped
2 cups cooked brown rice
1 cup milk
1 cup of cheddar cheese
2 teaspoons marjoram
2 teaspoons thyme
pinch red pepper flakes
salt and pepper

Directions: Blanch cauliflower and broccoli, drain. Sauté onions and mushrooms in a skillet until mushrooms are browned. Add to cauliflower and broccoli. To skillet add cup of milk and cup of cheddar cheese along with herbs. Cook to combine, and then mix into vegetables. Mix in cooked rice. Pour all into a baking dish, sprinkle on more cheddar cheese and cover the dish. Bake 45 minutes covered, then remove cover and bake another 15 minutes.
Bake at 350.

Smokey Cauliflower Poblano Gratin

Poblanos are my absolute favorite pepper! They are a bit spicy but not so much that you can't enjoy them. If your favorite farmer doesn't grow them you can usually find them in the specialty pepper section at the grocery store.

Ingredients:

1 large head (or two small heads) cauliflower, 3 pounds total

3 Tablespoons unsalted butter

3 Tablespoons flour

2 cups milk (I used whole milk)

Salt and pepper to taste

2 teaspoons smoked paprika

4 large poblano peppers, 1 pound total

Olive oil

12 ounces Parmesan, Asiago or Romano cheese, grated

Directions: Cut cauliflower into quarters and remove core. Cut into 1/4 inch slices. Blanch in boiling water for 3 minutes. Drain and rinse with cold water. Cut poblanos into quarters and remove seeds and stems. Place cut side down on a baking sheet and then press down with the palms of your hands to flatten poblanos. Brush with a little oil and then broil about 6 inches from heat until skins are very dark brown. Let cool and then remove skins and dice poblanos.

Preheat oven to 425 degrees.

Melt butter in a skillet over medium high heat. Whisk in flour until absorbed. Whisk in milk and simmer until thickened, about 2 to 3 minutes, whisking constantly. Stir in salt and pepper to taste. Stir in paprika. Layer as you would a lasagna in a 9 by 13 inch pan: 1/3 of cauliflower; 1/3 of poblanos; 2/3 cup of white sauce; and 1/3 of cheese; making three layers ending with cheese on top.

Bake for 25 to 30 minutes, until browned and bubbly around edges. Let stand 10 minutes before serving.

Butter-Crumbed Cauliflower

Ingredients:

1 large cauliflower

1 stick butter or margarine

1/4 cup fine bread crumbs

1 teaspoon chopped parsley

3 to 4 teaspoons grated Parmesan cheese

Directions: Wash and break the cauliflower into flowerets. Place in steamer or colander over water and steam, covered, for ten minutes, or cover with water and cook until just tender. While cauliflower is cooking, melt the butter or margarine, add the bread crumbs, and stir until lightly browned. Drain the flowerets and dip them in the hot bread mixture covering each completely. Place each in a casserole and pour the remaining bread crumb mixture over the cauliflower. Sprinkle with parsley and Parmesan cheese. Bake in a preheated 350° oven for 20 minutes. Serves 4 to 6.

Celeriac

Please don't judge this tasty vegetable by its appearance. Its rough exterior is not an accurate assumption of what lies inside. If you've ever asked a Midwestern farmer to grow celery they will tell you it's pretty hard. Our climate is not suited for the type of celery we are accustomed to seeing at the grocery store. Sad but true. I am a lover of celery. So this didn't sit well with me either. But then Hans grew celeriac! It's actually the root of the celery plant, and sometimes in recipes you'll see it referred to as celery root. The actual root has a wonderful celery-like flavor and can be eaten raw or cooked. Try peeling it, cutting it up and just eating it. Yum! The stalks and leaves that will sometimes accompany the root can be thrown in soup or a sauce for that same celery flavor. I freeze the leaves and stalks until it's time to make chicken stock.

Storing celeriac: Cut the tops off when you get it home, than wrap loosely in a cloth or bag and store in the crisper section. It should last about a month.

Preserving celeriac: The root lasts a really long time in the fridge, and you can freeze the tops like I suggested before or dry them to use as an herb. You can also dehydrate celeriac; just make sure you slice your pieces pretty thin.

Curried Celeriac Slaw

Ingredients:

1/2 cup dried tart cherries or cranberries

1/2 cup finely chopped red onion

3 Tablespoons plain yogurt

3 Tablespoons sour cream

1 Tablespoon Dijon mustard

1 teaspoon curry powder

1 teaspoon olive oil

1/2 teaspoon sugar

1/2 teaspoon salt

3 cups shredded, peeled celeriac (about 1 pound celery root)

Directions: Combine all ingredients except the celeriac in a large bowl, stirring with a whisk. Add celeriac; toss well to coat. Cover and chill 2 hours.

Apple and Celery Root Mash

Ingredients:

1/4 cup unsalted butter

1 3/4 Lbs. celeriac, peeled and cut into 1/2-inch cubes

2 medium, tart apples (such as Fuji or Braeburn), peeled, cored, and cut into 1/2-inch cubes

Salt, to taste

4 gratings of fresh nutmeg (fresh is best, however if all you have is pre-ground nutmeg than by all means... use it!)

1 star anise pod (optional)

1 cup apple cider

1/2 cup heavy (whipping) cream

Directions: Melt the butter in a large saucepan and add the celery root cubes. Cook over medium heat, stirring frequently, until the celery root starts to soften, about 15 minutes. Add the apples, salt, nutmeg, star anise, and apple cider, and bring the mixture to a simmer. Cover the pan and cook slowly until the mixture is very soft and tender, 45 to 60 minutes. Uncover and add the heavy cream. Cook until the cream is almost completely absorbed, about 10 minutes. Remove the pan from the heat and discard the star anise pod. Puree the mixture with an immersion or stick blender until it is smooth, or transfer the mixture to a food processor and process until smooth. The mash can be made a day in advance of serving. Cool completely and refrigerate, covered. To reheat, place in a small saucepan and cook over low heat, stirring frequently, until hot, 10 to 15 minutes.

French Celeriac Soup

Ingredients:

1 Tablespoon unsalted butter

1 yellow onion, finely sliced

1/4 pound boiling potatoes, peeled and cubed

1 3/4 pounds celery root, peeled and cubed

2 Tablespoons chopped fresh thyme

5 cups of vegetable stock

Salt

Freshly ground black pepper

Grated Gruyère cheese for serving (you could also use swiss)

Directions: In a large stockpot, melt the butter over medium heat until frothy. Add the onions, and cook on medium until caramelized, about 10 minutes. Add the potatoes, celery root, thyme, salt, pepper, and vegetable broth, and bring to a boil over high heat. Cover, and reduce the heat to medium-low, simmering for 30 minutes. Add the contents of the pot to a blender, and carefully purée until smooth or use an immersion blender or food mill. Serve hot, with a big pile of grated Gruyère to pile on top and melt into the soup.

Collard Greens

I'm going to be honest with you. I have very little experience cooking with collards. (Hanging my head in shame). Yet, I am very much aware of the amazing health benefits of collards and consume them because they really are a rocket ship to healthy eating. One cup of collards contain more than 500% of the daily value of vitamin K and A. Just one cup! They are great for your heart and digestive track and a packed full of cancer-fighting antioxidants. If you stumble upon collards consider it a blessing. Buy a bunch and get to eating!

Storing collards: Place unwashed collards in a bag and store in your crisper drawer.

Preserving collards: Blanch in boiling water for 3 minutes and then quickly submerge into an ice water bath. Drain and pack into freezer bags and store in the freezer.

Brown Lentil and Collard Soup

Ingredients:

1 yellow onion , chopped

3 tomatoes diced

2 Tablespoons of Olive Oil

1 bay leaf

3 large cloves garlic, minced

1 carrot, chopped

1 small zucchini , chopped

1 cup brown lentils

1.5 cups collard greens, chopped (center rib removed)

3 cups of water

3 cups of vegetable or chicken stock

1/2 teaspoon of cumin powder

2 teaspoons salt / or to taste

1/2 teaspoons of oregano

Directions: Heat oil in a large pot over medium heat. Sauté onions and garlic until translucent and tender. . Add carrots and zucchini and cook for few minutes. Add tomatoes, cumin powder, salt and bay leaf and cook for 2 minutes. Add brown lentils, oregano, collard greens, water and stock and cook for about 40-50 minutes until lentils are tender.

Collard Greens with Dumplings

Ingredients:

For the collard greens:

8 ounces bacon, diced

1 medium yellow onion, diced

3 medium garlic cloves, coarsely chopped

3 dried chipotle chiles

3/4 teaspoon kosher salt

1/4 teaspoon freshly ground black pepper

2 cups water

2 pounds collard greens, tough stems removed, washed, and cut into bite-sized pieces

For the dumplings:

1 cup all-purpose flour

1 teaspoon baking soda

3/4 teaspoon granulated sugar

1/4 teaspoon fine salt

1/2 cup well-shaken buttermilk

2 Tablespoons unsalted butter, melted and cooled slightly

Directions: For the collard greens: Place bacon in a 10-inch Dutch oven or a large, heavy-bottomed pot with a tight fitting lid over medium heat. Cook, stirring occasionally, until brown and crisp, about 15 to 20 minutes. Remove with a slotted spoon to a paper-towel-lined plate and discard all but 3 tablespoons of the bacon fat in the pot. Add onion, garlic, chiles, salt, and pepper and cook, stirring occasionally, until onion is tender and beginning to brown, about 8 to 10 minutes.

Add water, increase heat to high, and bring to a boil. Stir in greens a handful at a time, adding more as they wilt, until all are in the pot. Cover, reduce heat to low, and simmer, stirring occasionally, until greens are very tender and almost falling apart, about 30 minutes. Taste and season with additional salt and pepper as needed.

For the dumplings:

When the greens are ready, place the flour, baking soda, sugar, and salt in a medium bowl and whisk to combine. Add the buttermilk and melted butter and stir until the flour mixture is moistened and a soft dough forms.

Drop the dough in heaping tablespoons about 1/2 inch apart into the simmering greens. Cover and simmer until the dumplings are cooked through and the tops are no longer sticky, about 12 to 15 minutes. Remove the chipotle pods from the pot if desired. Sprinkle greens with reserved bacon and serve immediately.

Southern Style Collard Greens

Ingredients:

2 pounds of collard greens

1 ham hock or 6 slices of cooked bacon

1 medium onion, sliced or chopped

1 teaspoon of crushed red pepper

2 to 3 teaspoons Kosher salt

Directions: Clean and wash greens well; remove tough stems and ribs. Cut them up and place in a deep pot; add onion. Wash off ham hock and add to the pot. Add red pepper and salt. Add enough water to cover greens and cook until tender, about 1 hour. Taste and adjust seasonings. Serves 4 to 6.

Collard Cobbler with Cornmeal Biscuits

Cobbler doesn't have to be just for fruit!

Adapted from The Yellow House

Ingredients:

For the biscuits:

1 cup all-purpose flour

1/2 cup coarse yellow cornmeal

2 1/2 teaspoons baking powder

1 teaspoon honey

1/2 teaspoon salt

5 Tablespoons cold unsalted butter, cut into small pieces

3/4 cup buttermilk

For the collards:

About 1/2 pound Andouille sausage, halved lengthwise and sliced about 1/2-inch thick

1 large yellow onion, chopped

3 garlic cloves, minced

4 cups chicken stock or vegetable broth

3-4 pounds collard greens, thick stems removed and sliced into 1-inch ribbons

1/2 cup milk or cream

2 Tablespoons cornstarch dissolved in 1/4 cup water

salt and ground pepper

Directions: Make the biscuit dough: In a food processor, pulse flour, cornmeal, baking powder, salt, honey, and butter until the butter is in pieces about the size of small peas. Add the buttermilk and pulse until it forms a mass. Turn out the dough onto a floured surface, knead a few times. Roll the dough out about 3/4 to 1 inch thickness. Slice into square biscuits. Place the biscuits on a parchment-lined baking sheet in the refrigerator.

Sauté the sausage in a big pan until fat is rendered. If there doesn't seem to be much fat, add in a glug of olive oil. Add the onions and garlic and continue to sauté, stirring, until the onions are translucent. Add the broth and bring to a boil. Add the collards in batches, stirring after each addition. Lower the heat and simmer for approximately 30 minutes, until the mixture is reduced and collards are very tender.

Preheat oven to 375 degrees. Stir the milk and the cornstarch into the collard mixture, allowing it to simmer a bit more, uncovered, as it thickens up. Taste for salt and pepper and season if necessary.

Pour the entire mixture into an oven-safe glass dish. Remove the biscuits from the refrigerator, and lay them on top of the mixture, with the corners overlapping if possible. Grind black pepper over the biscuits. Bake the dish in the oven for 40-50 minutes, until biscuits are deep golden brown and collard mixture is bubbly.

Corn

Have you heard of the corn ear worm? I won't gross you out with details but those little suckers love to snack on sweet corn. The chemical applications that take care of the corn ear worm are very toxic and not something we'd ever apply to anything we grow, let alone eat something that's been doused in it. There are organic pesticides that we could use, however they don't work 100% of the time. If you love sweet corn and you'd prefer to eat organic sweet corn not all is lost. The corn worm usually only eats off the top inch of the cob... leaving a mealy brown mush. Just chop the top part off and you're good to go. The truth is, and this applies to all vegetables, if bugs don't want to eat it... why would you? If there's enough poison or lack of taste or nutrients to deter pests than it's probably not all that healthy or great tasting anyway.

In just my few years of farming I've come to find that

Midwesterners are ever consumed by two veggies come summer. I mean ADDICTED. Seriously in love with... willing to stand in a line 20 minutes long for... Tomatoes and sweet corn. It's very impressive the sheer quantity people pile into their carts or baskets. I think all farmers in the "corn-belt" should stop growing un-edible corn and soybeans and start growing sweet corn and tomatoes!

Storing corn: PUT YOUR CORN IN THE FRIDGE RIGHT NOW! Don't even finish reading this paragraph. Go. NOW!!!

Ok, glad you're back. So as I was saying... ever had tough, flavorless sweet corn? It could be that either the farmer didn't keep it cool right after harvest or you left it on the counter for a day before refrigerating it.

Preserving corn: I don't know of anyone that doesn't like summer sweet corn in the middle of January. Unless you're like my nephew Andy... who doesn't like corn at all (Can you imagine!?). You can freeze corn RIGHT ON THE COB! How easy is that? Corn can also be dehydrated for soups, and there are some really awesome canning recipes out there too. The hardest part of "putting up" corn is restraining yourself from eating it all before freezing/canning/dehydrating it!

Freezing Corn Right on the Cob:
There's debate on whether you need to blanch your ears of corn first before freezing. I always blanch because I feel like that sweet taste is preserved longer in the freezer. There are enzymes all vegetables have that, over time, break down and destroy nutrients and change the color, flavor, and texture of food during frozen storage. Blanching destroys those enzymes. So if you want to blanch, boil water, husk your corn, put the cobs in the boiling water

and blanch for 6-8 minutes. Remove and submerge into ice water to stop the cooking. Drain and pack in freezer bags. Later, when you are ready to serve the corn, it just takes about 5 or 6 minutes in a pot of boiling water. It doesn't need to be "cooked", just heated up!

Charred Corn Tacos with Zucchini-Radish Slaw

Adapted from www.smittenkitchen.com
Ingredients:
1/2 pound red radishes trimmed
1 small zucchini, long and narrow if you can find it
2 limes
Salt
4 ears corn, husks removed
2 Tablespoons unsalted butter
1 Tablespoon olive oil
1 medium white onion, finely chopped
2 cloves garlic, minced
3 Tablespoons chopped cilantro
1/2 cup crumbled queso fresco cheese (or another salty, crumbly cheese such as ricotta or feta)
1/4 teaspoon chili powder
10 to 12 small soft corn tortillas

Directions: Cut radishes and zucchini into tiny matchsticks with a mandoline. If you don't have a mandoline, you can use a peeler to peel thick ribbons down the long side of the zucchini. Stack the ribbons and cut them crosswise into thin matchsticks. Cut the radishes into a similar shape by hand. Toss radishes and zucchini together. Squeeze the juice of half a lime over the radish and season with salt. Add more lime juice if desired. Set aside.
Over a hot grill char two of the ears of corn until well-blackened but not completely burnt. Remove cobs from heat, and when cool enough to handle, shave off kernels using a large knife and reserve. Remove kernels from

remaining two ears of corn. Heat a large sauté pan over medium heat. Melt the butter and oil together and once hot, add the onion. Cook the onion for about 5 minutes, until softened. Add the garlic and cook another minute.

Add the raw corn kernels and sauté until corn is just cooked through, about three to five minutes. Turn heat to high, add the charred kernels of corn to the mixture, and toss to combine until heated through. Squeeze the juice of one lime over the corn mixture, and use the juice to scrape up any stuck bits. Season the corn mixture with salt and chili powder. Stir in chopped cilantro.

Heat your tortillas by wrapping the whole stack in foil and place it in a warm (250 degrees) oven for 15 minutes while you prepare the other ingredients.

Fill each taco with a few small spoonfuls of the corn mixture. Top with a spoonful of crumbled cheese and a bit of the radish-zucchini slaw. Serve with an extra lime wedge on the side (you'll have half a lime left to slice up), and whatever fixings you like (sour cream, avocado wedges, etc).

Mexican Grilled Corn

I know what you're going to say... "Mayonnaise??" But it's good. Really, really good.

Ingredients:

1/3 cup grated parmesan cheese

4 ears corn, husks and silk removed, cut in half

1 Tablespoon butter, room temperature

Salt and Pepper

2 Tablespoons mayonnaise (any kind you have in your fridge)

¼ teaspoon chili powder, chipotle or other

1 lime, cut into wedges for serving

Directions: Heat grill to high. Place cheese on a plate or in a shallow bowl; set aside. Brush corn with butter, and season to taste. Grill, turning every 2-3 minutes, until tender and slightly charred, 10-12 minutes; let cool 2-3 minutes Brush corn with mayo, and roll in cheese to coat. Sprinkle with chili powder; serve with lime.

Herbed Sweet Corn and Tomato Salad

This is great to take to picnics and BBQs!

Ingredients:

6 ears fresh sweet corn, shucked

4 medium tomatoes, as ripe as possible

½ of a medium red onion, diced

1/4 cup (or small handful) fresh mint leaves

1/4 cup (or small handful) fresh mixed herbs — like Italian parsley, basil, rosemary, sage

1 Tablespoon olive oil

Salt and fresh black pepper, to taste

3 ounces soft goat cheese, chilled and crumbled

Directions: Bring a large pot of water to boil over medium-high heat. Add the corn and boil for five minutes. Drain and let cool. Meanwhile, roughly dice the tomatoes and onion.

When the corn has cooled, stand each ear up in a wide, shallow bowl and slice the corn kernels off with a chef's knife. Toss the corn with the tomatoes and onion.

Finely mince the mint and herb leaves and toss with the vegetables, along with the olive oil. Season to taste with salt and pepper, then crumble in the goat cheese and toss gently. Serve and enjoy!

Note: Of course this is good with many other mix-ins too; we added a few cubes of grilled eggplant to this salad. Sometimes we like avocado and lime juice or a splash of balsamic vinegar and some dried oregano.

Sweet Corn Soup

Want a vegan option... see the next recipe.

Ingredients:

6 ears of corn, kernels cut off the cobs, kernels reserved

6 slices of bacon, diced

2 large yellow onions, diced

3 garlic cloves, minced

1/4 teaspoon of red pepper flakes

Kosher salt and freshly ground black pepper, to taste

1/4 cup heavy cream

Directions: In a 5-quart Dutch oven over medium-high heat, cook the bacon until crisp, about 8 minutes. Using a slotted spoon, transfer to a paper towel-lined plate. Finely chop the bacon; set aside. Discard all but 2 Tbs. of the fat from the pot. Set the pot over medium heat, add the onions and cook, stirring occasionally, until the onions are soft and translucent, 6 to 7 minutes. Add the garlic and red pepper flakes and cook, stirring constantly, about 30 seconds. Add the corn kernels and cook, stirring occasionally, until the corn is softened, about 10 minutes. Add the reserved corn juices and 7 cups water, and season with salt and black pepper. Increase the heat to medium-high and bring to a boil. Reduce the heat to medium-low and simmer for 20 minutes.Using a food processor, blend the soup in batches until smooth. Return the soup to the pot and stir in the cream. Adjust the seasonings with salt and black pepper. Ladle the soup into warmed bowls and garnish with the bacon. Serve immediately. Serves 8 to 10.

Corn and Bell Pepper Vegan Soup Recipe
Ingredients:
2 Tablespoons of olive oil
1 red onion, finely chopped
2 cups finely chopped bell peppers
3 cloves garlic, finely chopped
6 ears of corn, kernels cut off the cobs, kernels reserved
4 cups vegetable stock
4 sprigs thyme (additional to garnish)
1/4 teaspoon of crushed red pepper flakes
1 teaspoon of salt
1/8 teaspoon of fresh ground pepper

Directions: Heat olive oil in a large pot on medium high. Add red onion, bell peppers and garlic. Stir to coat and cook 3-5 minutes until softened. Add corn and stir again, let cook another 3 minutes.
Add vegetable stock and leaves from four thyme sprigs and bring to a boil. Reduce heat and let simmer 10 minutes. Remove 2 cups of the soup and puree with an immersion blender. Add red pepper flakes, kosher salt and fresh ground pepper to the puree.
Return puree to the soup pot and stir. Serve garnished with fresh thyme.

Cucumbers

There are very few vegetables Hans won't eat. Cucumbers are one of those. This drives me nuts because I love them. If the skin is soft enough I'll just pick one from the field and eat the whole thing right there on the spot. Whenever I make something with cucumbers it's pretty much a guarantee I will be the only one eating it. Recently, we went to the wine bar in downtown Bloomington called A Renee. They served cucumber water. It's an amazing alternative to putting a lemon or lime in your water and I thought it was even more refreshing! They didn't actually place any cucumbers in the water when serving it, therefore Hans had no idea and ended up drinking at least a pitcher full!

Storing cucumbers: Cucumbers should be stored in the refrigerator where they will keep for several days. If you do not use the entire cucumber during one meal, place it in a tightly sealed container so that it does not become dried out.

Preserving cucumbers: Pickles anyone? There are many tasty recipes out there for canning pickles and I highly suggest you try one sometime. But there's also something called freezer pickles. Same great taste, but no canning required! They can even be stored in the fridge for up to 4 months!

Old Timey Freezer Pickles

Ingredients:

5 small cucumbers, washed & thinly sliced

1 large onion, peeled & thinly sliced

1/2 cup cider vinegar

1/2 teaspoon of salt

1/2 cup honey

1/2 cup water

2 cloves of garlic (crushed)

8 sprigs of fresh dill

Directions: Invest in some freezer containers. They usually are a semi-clear plastic with a light blue lid. I get mine at Farm n Fleet but they are available in the canning section alongside the mason jars. Layer the cucumbers & onions in the freezer containers. Whisk together the vinegar, salt, honey, water & garlic until well combined. Pour over the cucumbers & onions leaving about 1 inch of headroom (it will expand when it freezes). Top with the sprigs of dill. Cover & freeze.

Back to that cucumber water... so I decided to try my own. I added some extra stuff. It was amazing! I'll be sipping this all summer!

Katie's Cucumber Water

Prepare it the day before you start to enjoy it.

Ingredients:

1 cucumber, sliced and unpeeled + 6-7 cucumber slices for decoration

1 1/2 to 2 liters of water

3 mint sprigs + 2 mint sprigs for decoration

Half a lemon, sliced and unpeeled

Ice cubes

Directions: In a pitcher, mix the water, cucumber, 3 mint sprigs and lemon. Let it rest on the fridge for 24 hours. If you prepare the water at the last minute, cut the first cucumber in three or four pieces. Then, squeeze the cucumber pieces to release all the juice.

Before serving remove the cucumber slices used to flavor the water. Then stir with a wooden spoon, add some ice cubes, 6 or 7 fresh cucumber slices and the remaining 2 mint sprigs.

Cucumber and Tomato Salad

This is my "go-to" recipe when we're having big dinners at the farm. It's super easy to make and we're usually up to our ears in tomatoes and cucumbers. I haven't met an intern or farmhand that didn't go back for seconds.

Ingredients:

2 large tomatoes, diced

1 medium cucumber, diced

½ red onion, diced

2 Tablespoons of balsamic vinegar

2 Tablespoons of olive oil

A sprig or two of basil, chopped

1 clove of garlic, minced

Salt and pepper to taste

½ cup of crumbled feta cheese (optional)

Directions: place died vegetables and basil in a bowl. Whisk vinegar, oil, garlic, salt and pepper and pour over vegetables. Gently stir in feta. Cover, and let stand in refrigerator for at least 30 minutes until ready to serve. Tastes fantastic if left in overnight.

Cucumber Raita

A great Indian condiment! Serve with fish or chicken,
great just plain with pita or naan!

Ingredients:

2 pints thick yogurt (recommended: Greek yogurt)

1/2 bunch cilantro leaves, chopped

1 lemon, juiced

Salt and freshly ground black pepper

2 cucumbers, peeled, seeded and chopped

2 tablespoons chopped mint leaves

Directions: Put the yogurt, cilantro, lemon juice, and salt
and pepper, to taste, into a blender and puree until the
mixture is smooth and green. Pour it into a bowl and fold in
the cucumber and mint. Refrigerate at least 1/2 hour
before serving to allow the flavors to develop. Taste and
adjust the seasoning before serving.

E

Eggplant

Eggplant can be an intimidating vegetable. Don't let it
intimidate you. Try to forget all the times that soggy,
tasteless eggplant left you disappointed. You must purge
these memories before you can move on and start enjoying
this wonderful vegetable. Hold my hand... it will be alright.
The key is finding a recipe that works and lucky for you I
have some so read on and get ready to be liberated from
your eggplant anxieties!

Storing eggplant: Uncut eggplants will stay fresh for about
a week in the refrigerator. Be sure to place them carefully
without cutting or scrapping the skin. The skin is an

important part of the plant that keeps them fresh for a longer period of time either in or out of the refrigerator. If the skin isn't cut you can also store eggplant on your counter for a day or so.

Preserving eggplant: From my experience, freezing eggplant is possible but just turns into mush. I'd suggest freezing the dish you've made with eggplant. There's lots of talk on the internet about submerging eggplant and garlic in olive oil and keeping it for up to a year. It's possible, but there is a risk of botulism. Just be warned.

Grilled Eggplant

For all you eggplant newbies out there:
Ingredients:
1 eggplant
3 Tablespoons olive oil
3 Tablespoons balsamic vinegar
2 Tablespoons minced garlic
Dash of oregano
Dash of thyme
Salt
Freshly ground black pepper

Directions: Mix all the ingredients together except the eggplant. Cut the eggplant lengthwise into 1/2 inch thick slices. Brush the sliced eggplant on both sides with the marinade mixture. Let sit for 5 minutes. Brush again with the mixture and place on a hot grill. Grill for 7 minutes and flip. Grill for another 7 minutes and serve.

Grilled Eggplant and Olive Pizza

Adapted from Gourmet magazine, 2009

Ingredients:

1 garlic clove, minced

1/3 cup extra-virgin olive oil

1 1/4 pound eggplant, cut into 3/4-inch-thick rounds

1 pound store-bought pizza or homemade pizza dough at room temperature

5 ounces sliced provolone, shredded (if you can't find shredded provolone you can use fresh mozzarella too).

A handful of pitted green olives, coarsely chopped (1/3 cup)

1/4 cup chopped flat-leaf parsley

Directions: To make this pizza on a grill, or in a grill pan: Stir together garlic and oil. Brush some of garlic oil on both sides of eggplant and season with 3/4 teaspoon salt and 1/2 teaspoon pepper. Grill over direct medium heat, covered, turning once, until tender, 6 to 8 minutes total. Cut into roughly one-inch pieces and set aside.

Stretch dough or pizza crust into about a 12- by 10-inch rectangle (or into the shape of your grill pan, which in my case, was round) on a large baking sheet or your counter and lightly brush with garlic oil. Oil grill rack, then put dough, oiled side down, on grill. Brush top with more garlic oil. Grill, covered, until underside is golden-brown, about 2 to 3 minutes.

Using tongs, return crust, grilled side up, to baking sheet. Scatter eggplant, cheese, olives, and parsley (whoops, forgot mine) over crust. Slide pizza from sheet onto grill and grill, covered, until underside is golden-brown and cheese is melted, about 3 to 5 minutes. (If you're using an oven-safe grill pan, you can slide the pan into a preheated 500 degree oven at this point; which gets the toppings that much more blistered.) Season to taste with salt, pepper and a red pepper flakes.

To make this pizza in the oven: You can either fry or roast the eggplant slices, brushed with garlic oil, until tender. Prepare the pizza as you would any other, rolling or stretching out the dough, mounding on the toppings and sliding it onto a baking sheet or pizza stone in an oven that has been preheated to its top temperature. It will be ready in about 10 minutes.

Ratatouille
Big word. Big taste.
Ingredients:
1/4 cup olive oil, plus more as needed
1 1/2 cups small diced yellow onion
1 teaspoon minced garlic
2 cups medium diced eggplant, skin on
1/2 teaspoon fresh thyme leaves
1 cup diced red bell peppers
1 cup diced zucchini squash
1 cup diced yellow squash
1 1/2 cups peeled, seeded and chopped tomatoes
1 Tablespoon thinly sliced fresh basil leaves
1 Tablespoon chopped fresh parsley leaves
Salt and freshly ground black pepper

Directions: Set a large sauté pan over medium heat and add the olive oil. Once hot, add the onions and garlic to the pan. Cook the onions, stirring occasionally about 5 to 7 minutes. Add the eggplant and thyme to the pan and continue to cook, stirring occasionally, until the eggplant is partially cooked, about 5 minutes.

Add the red peppers, zucchini, and squash and continue to cook for an additional 5 minutes. Add the tomatoes, basil, parsley, and salt and pepper, to taste, and cook for a final 5 minutes. Stir well to blend and serve either hot or at room temperature.

Roasted Eggplant Spread

Adapted from Barefoot Contessa
If you don't like the consistency of eggplant, give this spread a try! It's great on bread, crackers, etc.
Ingredients:
1 medium eggplant
2 red bell peppers, seeded
1 red onion, peeled
2 garlic cloves, minced
3 Tablespoons good olive oil
1 1/2 teaspoons salt
1/2 teaspoon ground black pepper
2 Tablespoons tomato paste
1 teaspoon of dried oregano
½ cup of grated parmesan cheese (optional)

Directions: Preheat the oven to 400 degrees. Cut the eggplant, bell pepper, and onion into 1-inch cubes. Toss them in a large bowl with the garlic, olive oil, oregano, parmesan, salt, and pepper. Spread them on a baking sheet. Roast for 45 minutes, until the vegetables are lightly browned and soft, tossing once during cooking.
Cool slightly.

Place the vegetables in a food processor with the steel blade, add the tomato paste, and pulse 3 or 4 times to blend.

F

Fennel

Surprisingly, fennel isn't a big seller at the farmers market. I think the problem is most people don't know what to do with it. Before Hans and I started farming I never bought fennel so I understand folk's apprehension. But I'm here to say that fennel is a versatile and easy-to-prepare vegetable! There are recipes that focus on fennel as the star ingredient but fennel is also great in a supporting role! For instance, when making soup I sauté my carrots, celery and onions with a bulb of chopped fennel. Shaved fennel is great on salads. Hans and I really enjoy roasting potatoes and fennel in the oven (roasting fennel makes it super sweet!). When we travelled to Italy there were baskets full of fennel at the grocery store so we grabbed some and sautéed them with tomatoes in our apartment kitchen. It was incredibly simple and tasty!

Storing fennel: You can store fresh fennel in the refrigerator crisper where it should keep fresh for about 7-10 days. Yet, it is best to consume fennel soon after purchase since as it ages, it tends to gradually lose its flavor.

Preserving fennel: You can blanch and freeze fennel but it rapidly loses its flavor. There are some really good pickling recipes for fennel for canning. I've done some research and many recipes say it's ok it process in a water bath, but for the safest results use a pressure canner.

Scalloped Potatoes with Fennel

Ingredients:

2 pounds yukon gold potatoes

2 medium fennel bulbs

1 medium onion

2 cups heavy cream

4 Tablespoons of melted butter

1 1/2 cup chicken broth

3 Tablespoons flour

1 teaspoon pepper

1/4 teaspoon grated nutmeg

3 cloves garlic, minced

Directions: Preheat oven to 400 degrees. Peel potatoes and slice into 1/8 inch slices using a mandolin or very sharp knife. Divide into three piles and set aside. Chop off the frilly tops of the fennel bulb and save for another use. Slice off the root end of the bulb and discard, and then thinly cut the fennel into 1/4 inch slices. Peel onion, cut off root end and discard, then cut onion into 1/4 inch slices. In a medium bowl, whisk together cream, broth, flour, pepper, nutmeg and garlic. In a greased, 2-quart casserole dish, layer one portion of the potatoes. Top with a half of the fennel and onions. Add another layer of potatoes. Season lightly with salt and pepper. Pour in half of the cream mixture. Layer on the rest of the fennel and onions and top with the remaining potato slices. Season lightly with salt and pepper and pour over the remaining cream mixture, pressing down to temporarily immerse the top layer. Drizzle the top with melted butter, place on a baking sheet with sides (in case it bubbles over) and put in the oven to bake for one hour, or until potatoes are golden brown on the top and tender when pierced with a knife.

Shaved Fennel Salad

Ingredients:

1 fennel bulb, shaved paper thin with a mandolin or the side of a box grater

2 Tablespoons of extra virgin olive oil

1 Tablespoons of fresh lemon juice

1/8 teaspoon of chopped fresh thyme leaves

1 Tablespoons chopped flat-leafed parsley

2 Tablespoons shaved Parmesan cheese

Directions: Mix all ingredients together. It tastes better when chilled for an hour or so.

Penne with Fennel Pesto

This dish uses those frilly fronds on the tops of the fennel tops. It's great when you've used the bulb of the fennel for a separate dish but don't know what to do with those fronds!

1/3 cup pistachios, toasted

2-3 cloves garlic, peeled and roughly chopped

1 ounce (about ½ cup) freshly grated Parmesan

1 teaspoon salt, plus more for pasta water

Ground black pepper, to taste

2 cups fennel fronds (usually from 2 fennel bulbs)

4-5 mint leaves, torn (optional)

about ½ cup extra virgin olive oil

juice of ½ lemon, or to taste

1 pound penne pasta

1 cup frozen peas

Directions: Put the pistachios, garlic, cheese, salt, and pepper in a food processor. Pulse a few times to grind slightly. Add fennel and mint to the food processor. With the motor running, drizzle in the olive oil until the mixture is reduced to a paste and has a spreadable, but not greasy consistency. Taste and add salt if necessary. Squeeze in a little bit of lemon juice to taste. Bring a large pot of water to a boil. Salt the water generously and cook the pasta until al dente. While the pasta is cooking, set up a colander in the sink and put the frozen peas in it. (If you have fresh peas, by all means use them. You can add them to the boiling water in the last few minutes of cooking the pasta.) When the pasta is done, drain the pasta in the colander. Return the pasta, along with the peas, into the pot. Stir in the pesto until pasta is lightly coated and flavorful. Squeeze in a little lemon juice, to taste. Serve hot or at room temperature.

White Bean Fennel Soup
Ingredients:
1 large onion, chopped
1 small fennel bulb, thinly sliced
1 Tablespoon olive oil
5 cups reduced-sodium chicken broth or vegetable broth
1 can (15 ounces) white kidney or cannellini beans, rinsed and drained
1 can (14-1/2 ounces) diced tomatoes, undrained (feel free to use 3 average tomatoes diced instead of canned tomatoes!)
1 teaspoon dried thyme
1/4 teaspoon pepper
1 bay leaf
3 cups shredded fresh spinach

Directions: In a large saucepan, sauté onion and fennel in oil until tender. Add the broth, beans, tomatoes, thyme, pepper and bay leaf; bring to a boil. Reduce heat; cover and simmer for 30 minutes or until fennel is tender. Discard bay leaf. Add spinach; cook 3-4 minutes longer or until spinach is wilted.

Roasted Cauliflower, Onion & Fennel

Ingredients:

1 medium head of cauliflower (about 1 1/4 pounds), cored, cut into 1-inch florets

6 Tablespoons olive oil, divided

2 medium onions (about 1/2 pound each), halved lengthwise, cut into 3/4-inch-wide wedges with some core still attached, peeled

2 fresh fennel bulbs (about 1 pound total), halved lengthwise, cut lengthwise into 1/2-inch-wide wedges with some core still attached

8 small garlic cloves, unpeeled

2 Tablespoons of oregano

Directions: Position rack in center of oven; preheat to 425°F. Toss cauliflower and 2 tablespoons oil in large bowl. Heat heavy large skillet over medium-high heat. Add cauliflower and sauté until beginning to brown, about 5 minutes. Transfer cauliflower to rimmed baking sheet.

Add 2 tablespoons oil to same skillet. Add onion wedges. Cook until browned on 1 side, about 3 minutes. Using spatula, carefully transfer onions to baking sheet with cauliflower, arranging wedges browned side up. Add remaining 2 tablespoons oil to same skillet. Add fennel; sauté until fennel softens slightly and starts to brown, about 5 minutes. Transfer to same baking sheet.

Scatter garlic and oregano over vegetables. Sprinkle with salt and pepper. Roast until vegetables are caramelized, about 25 minutes. Serve hot or at room temperature.

G

Garlic

Garlic, Green Garlic and Garlic Scapes...
It's pretty amazing that one single plant can produce so much awesomeness! I've included garlic scapes and green garlic into the same section as garlic because it's all from the same plant and it's just easier. What's a garlic scape you ask? Scapes are the part of the garlic plant that, if left to its own will, would flower. As farmers we don't want the garlic plant to flower because it takes up too much energy and then you get smaller garlic bulbs. As eaters you don't want the plant to flower because eating garlic scapes is an exciting taste excursion that only happens a few weeks out of the year. The scapes are a lot like green onions, but a little crunchier and with a pleasing garlic taste. Cook with them, dry them and add to soups and stews, puree them for sauces or pesto or eat them raw diced into a salad. So that's the scapes. What about green garlic? That's really easy. Green garlic is just a very young garlic plant. Sometimes called "spring garlic," it's produces long shoots of edible leaves and a small tender garlic clove at the end. With green garlic you use the WHOLE thing. Leaves and bulb. Use the leaves in place of anything you'd use a scallion or green onion and the bulb just like regular garlic cloves. It's another short-lived treat so enjoy them while you have them!

Storing Garlic: The entire garlic bulb is best stored in a cool, dark place. It will last a long time. Months and months and months. Garlic scapes last a week or two in the fridge. Just keep in a bag and place in the crisper. Green garlic is the most perishable. The cloves will last longer than the leaves. Expect maybe a week for the leaves. Keep in the fridge as well.

Preserving Garlic: Since garlic bulbs last so long, it's really unnecessary to preserve them. Garlic scapes and green garlic are a little different. We make garlic scape pesto in HUGE batches and freeze it. See the recipe below. If you like garlic you'll love this pesto. It's got a big garlic kick! Freezing scapes whole doesn't allow for a great texture but you could dice them, freeze and then add to soups and sauces as a nice replacement for garlic. We dry ours in a food dehydrator and it works lovely. Green garlic is a little trickier to preserve. It doesn't like freezing and drying it can deplete a lot of flavor. I say just dig into it... use it in everything and enjoy it while you can!

Garlic Scape Pesto:
Ingredients:
2/3 cup garlic scapes, chopped
1/3 cup pine nuts or walnuts (if you'd prefer not to use nuts that's ok too)
1/3 cup grated Parmesan cheese
1/3 cup olive oil
Salt, pepper to taste
Directions: In a food processor place garlic scapes, nuts, and Parmesan. Set to low and drizzle the oil in slowly as the processor is running.

Garlic Scape Hummus

Ingredients:

1/3 cup sliced garlic scapes

1 Tablespoon lemon juice

½ teaspoon salt

Black pepper (to taste)

1 can (15-ounces) cannellini beans, rinsed and drained

¼ cup olive oil

Directions: In the bowl of a food processor, process the garlic scapes, lemon juice, salt and black pepper until finely chopped, scraping the sides as needed.

Add the beans and process to a rough puree (the beans will be just about completely mashed).

With the machine running, slowly pour in the olive oil and process until smooth. Check the consistency; if it is still thick and paste-like, you can add 2 or 3 tablespoons of water to thin it out a bit. Taste, and add more salt and pepper, if desired. Serve with your favorite vegetables, pita chips, etc.

Homemade Butter with Green Garlic

Fresh butter, green garlic and a touch of parsley: Bread has never been so happy!

Ingredients:

two stalks green garlic

1/4 cup fresh parsley

1/2 teaspoon salt

1 pint heavy cream

Directions: Wash and trim the ends off the green garlic stalks. You want to use as much of it as possible, including the green stem, but you'll have to take at least one layer off the outside to get it clean. Cut into 2-inch lengths and place in the bowl of a food processor with the parsley. Process until finely minced. Add the salt and the cream to the food processor and turn it on. Let the mixture whirl about 5 minutes, until you see the curds and whey separate. The curds are the butter; the whey you want to drain off. I tossed my whey, but if you can think of a use for it, save it - it's basically garlic-flavored buttermilk. Scoop the curds lightly into a sieve lined with cheesecloth or a paper coffee filter. Let drain at least two hours, or even overnight. You may have to press the curds and knead them to get out the excess liquid. You'll be left with a soft, smooth butter. Spread liberally on good bread, add to cooked pasta or use it to top grilled steak.

Green Garlic Pasta

Ingredients:
1 Tablespoon of olive oil
2 Tablespoons of butter
15 stalks of green garlic
good pinch salt
½ cup vegetable stock
1 bunch fresh spinach
¼ cup of cream
Box of linguine or fettuccine

Directions: Slice the green garlic into thin pieces. Heat olive oil and butter in a skillet, add the garlic and salt, and cover the pan. Cook for about 10 minutes, until it begins to release a sweet and mellow aroma. Add the vegetable stock, bring to a boil, reduce heat again and simmer, covered, for another fifteen minutes. Add the spinach, cover the pan, turn up the heat and cook for a couple of minutes, until the spinach is dark green and just wilted. Turn off the heat and, working in batches, puree the garlic-spinach mixture in a food processor. Return to the pan, add the cream, and heat gently. Add more salt to taste. Toss with hot pasta and serve with grated Parmesan.

Creamy Green Garlic Soup (A nice vegan option!)
Russets or baking potatoes are the best for soups like this
due to their high starch content. Yukons have a medium
starch content and will also work well, while adding a
touch of their "buttery" feel.
Ingredients:
2 Tablespoons Olive Oil or Dairy-Free Margarine (I used
olive oil)
1 Medium Onion, diced (about 1-1/4 cups)
1/2 lb Green Garlic or 3 bulbs, thinly sliced and cut in half
(I used the whites & part way up the green) – can sub 2 to
4 minced medium garlic cloves
1/2 lb Yukon Gold or Russet Potatoes, cut into 1/2-inch
cubes (I didn't peel)
1/2 teaspoon Salt, plus more to taste (I used 1 teaspoon
total)
1 Quart vegetable Broth

Directions: Heat the oil or margarine in a stockpot over
medium heat. Add the onions and sauté for 3 to 5 minutes,
or until they begin to soften and become translucent.
Add the garlic, potatoes, and 1/2 teaspoon of salt, and
sauté for another 5 minutes – keeping things moving. If the
pan dries out, splash in a bit of the broth to keep the
ingredients from sticking.

Add the broth and bring the soup to a boil. Cover and
reduce the heat to medium-low, allowing the soup to
simmer for about 20 minutes, or until the potatoes are nice
and tender.

Using an immersion blender, or in two batches in a regular
blender, puree the soup (garlic, onions, potatoes and all)
until it is nice and smooth. I did it in my blender, allowing
each batch to spin for a couple of minutes. Use caution
when you turn the blender on, making sure you have a firm

hand on the lid to ensure that no hot soup escapes. Trust me, that is never fun!

Return the soup to your pot and season with additional salt and freshly ground black pepper to taste.

Farmhand Hummus

I call this "Farmhand hummus" because whenever I feed it to our farm helpers it completely disappears! I love making it for them because all of the protein really keeps them satisfied and full of energy and I can do it the night before. I serve it with bread, pita, veggies or on sandwiches.

Ingredients:

2 cans garbanzo beans

2-3 cloves of garlic 4 Tablespoons of tahini

1 ½ teaspoons salt

Pinch of cumin

¼ teaspoon of pepper

1 Tablespoon chopped parsley (optional)

Dash or two of paprika. 1/4 cup olive oil, 2 lemons, juiced (I've used oranges before and it turned out really, really good)

Directions: In food processor fitted with the steel blade attachment add everything but the olive oil. Turn food processor on low and slowly add the olive oil through the spout until creamy. Store covered in the fridge.

K

Kale

Kale is a powerhouse. It's a super-veggie packed with nutrients. It's been touted as the "Queen of Greens." It's one of the most nutrient-dense foods out there. You want to eat healthy? Eat Kale. Here's why: One cup of kale contains 5 grams of fiber, 180% of vitamin A, 200% of vitamin C, and 1,020% of vitamin K. It is also a good source of minerals copper, potassium, iron, manganese, and phosphorus.

Using kale in your day-to-day cooking is really easy. Eat it raw in salads, throw it any soup (it's pretty awesome in tomato or minestrone!), casserole, smoothie, stir-fry, sauce or egg dish. Toss with pasta, olive oil and fresh tomatoes. I use it whenever I make lasagna. Kale pesto is really great too, and you can freeze it to use later. Try different varieties like Lacinato kale or Red Russian. They all taste a bit different!

Storing Kale: Wrap your unwashed kale in a bag and store it in the crisper drawer. It should keep for 5 days or so.

Preserving Kale: Easiest way is to freeze it just like other greens. Wash it, cut out that center rib and stem. Blanch it for 2 minutes; submerge in ice water and drain to dry. Place in freezer bags and store flat in the freezer.

Baked Kale Chips

Ingredients:

1 medium bunch kale

1 Tablespoon olive oil

Salt, to taste

Directions: Preheat oven to 300°F. Rinse and dry the kale, then remove the stems and tough center ribs. Cut into large pieces, toss with olive oil in a bowl then sprinkle with salt. Arrange leaves in a single layer on a large baking sheet. Bake for 10-15 minutes, or until crisp. Place baking sheet on a rack to cool. Keep a close eye and check every couple of minutes or so. The key to good kale chips is not to overcook (than they taste super salty and bitter) but not to undercook (than they aren't crisp... duh). So I suggest doing a test run and keeping track of how long it takes in your oven.

Kale Shake

I was given this recipe from my fantastic chiropractors at Healthy Living Family Chiropractic in Bloomington, Illinois. They got it from Dr. Axe. It's a great way to get a ton of nutrients in when you're on the go or if you're a little weary of eating your greens (It's sweet and delicious!).

Ingredients:

1/2 bunch kale

1 banana

1/4 cup red grapes

1 teaspoon of vanilla

1 teaspoon of cinnamon

1 dash cayenne pepper (to taste)

1/2 cup ice

1/2 cup water (or until consistency is reached)

Directions: Put all the ingredients into a blender and blend until smooth.

Kale Salad

CSA Member Leann Steidinger
Ingredients:
A bunch of Kale
Mandarin oranges, reserve the juice (no sugar added is best)
White wine vinegar
Ground pepper
Slivered almonds

Directions: whisk mandarin orange juice with vinegar and pepper. Pour over kale and top with slivered almonds.

Braised Kale & Garlic

This is a super easy way to make kale as a great side dish!
Ingredients:
1 Tablespoon olive oil
1 1/2 cups thinly sliced onion
1/3 cup thinly sliced garlic
10 cups loosely packed chopped kale (about 2 pounds)
1 cup of chicken or vegetable stock
1 cup water
3/4 teaspoon crushed red pepper
2 teaspoons red wine vinegar
1/4 teaspoon salt
1/4 teaspoon black pepper

Directions: Heat olive oil in a large sauté pan over medium heat. Add onion and garlic; cook 10 minutes or until golden, stirring frequently. Add kale, broth, 1 cup water, and red pepper; cover and bring to a boil. Reduce heat, and simmer 20 minutes. Stir in vinegar, salt, and black pepper.

Zuppa Tuscano Soup

(A copycat version of Olive Garden's)
The Pioneer Woman copied Olive Garden and I'm copying
The Pioneer Woman. This makes a ton.

Ingredients:

2 bunches kale, washed and center rib and stem removed
12 whole potatoes, sliced thin (leave the skin on!)
1 onion, chopped
1-1/2 pound Italian sausage
1/2 teaspoon red pepper flakes
2 cups chicken broth
2 cups whole milk
4 cups half-and-half
dried oregano
1 teaspoon of salt
black pepper to taste

Directions: In a medium pot. boil sliced potatoes until
tender. Drain and set aside.

In a large pot, crumble and brown the Italian sausage. Add
the onion and cook until translucent. Drain as much as the
fat as you can. Stir in the red pepper flakes, oregano, salt,
chicken broth, milk, and half-and-half. Simmer for 30
minutes.

Give it a taste and adjust seasonings as needed. Add the
potatoes then stir in the kale. Simmer an additional 10-15
minutes, then serve.

Pasta with Kale & Roasted Tomatoes

Ingredients:

1 lb spaghetti

1 large bunch of kale, trimmed from thick stalk and thinly sliced

2 pints cherry tomatoes

2 Tablespoons olive oil

Salt and pepper, sprinkle

4 cloves garlic

Salt and pepper, to taste

Pinch red chili flakes, optional

Directions: Preheat oven to 350°F. Place cherry tomatoes on a parchment-lined baking sheet. Toss with 1 tablespoon of olive oil and sprinkle with salt and pepper. Roast in preheated oven for 20 minutes until nicely caramelized and shriveled up. Set aside.

Bring a large pot of water to boil over high heat. Cook pasta according to package directions. Meanwhile, heat second amount of olive oil in a large deep skillet over medium heat. Add garlic and sauté 1 minute. Add kale and toss to coat in olive oil. Cook down until just wilted.

Drain cooked pasta and add to the skillet. Toss with the kale mixture. Add roasted cherry tomatoes at the end and toss gently to prevent breaking up the tomatoes too much. Add chili flakes, if using and season with salt and pepper if needed.

made w/ whole wheat pasta
ground pork
black-eyed peas

Shells With White Beans, Kale and Bacon

Ingredients

8 oz. box of pasta shells (small shells or macaroni will work).

4 to 6 slices bacon, chopped

2 cups chopped onion

1 celery stalk, chopped

3 cups chopped chard

1 cup low-sodium chicken or other stock

3 cups cooked or canned cannellini or other white beans, drained but still moist

salt & ground black pepper

Freshly grated Parmesan cheese for garnish

Directions: Bring a large pot of water to a boil over high heat and salt it. Add the pasta and cook until tender but not mushy, 8 to 10 minutes; drain and set aside.

While the pasta is cooking, place the bacon in a large skillet over medium-high heat. Once the bacon begins to color, add the onion and celery and cook until just soft, then add the chard and cook until the bacon is done. Add stock and beans, and sprinkle with salt and pepper; cook until heated through, about 5 more minutes. If it seems dry, add a little more stock or water; it should be moist but not soupy. Add the pasta to the bean mixture and stir gently. Taste and adjust the seasoning, sprinkle with Parmesan.

Goat Cheese Kale

CSA Member Kathryn Foster

Ingredients:

One bunch of fresh kale (Rinsed, large stems cut out and roughly chopped)

2 Tablespoons of Olive Oil

Fresh ground pepper to taste

Balsamic Vinegar

Goat cheese

Directions: Cover the bottom of the heated skillet with olive oil and heat it up. Grind fresh pepper into the skillet and heat. Add kale and sauté for 3-5 minutes. The kale will cook down a bit. Toss occasionally to prevent burning. Sprinkle balsamic vinegar over the sautéed kale, turn off burner and cover the pan. Crumble goat cheese to taste and add to the pan. Plate, pour any liquid left in the pan over the kale and serve.

This works for any kind of greens.

Kohlrabi

What looks like an alien but tastes really, really good? Kohlrabi! This crazy vegetable is sometimes compared to a cross between a cabbage and turnip. If it's fresh it's really great raw. Just peel and use on a veggie tray or shave it onto a salad or slaw. Hans' dad Dave likes to pan fry it with a bit of olive oil, garlic and salt and pepper. It's great in stir-fries, roasted, thrown in soups; regardless of how you can prepare it, don't let it's funky look fool you. It's a tasty treat! Something really noteworthy about this veg is it's leaves are PACKED with vitamin C. Ridiculous amounts. Hans and I have juiced the leaves before (not very appetizing plain but an apple and carrot will help with that!). The leaves are edible, so enjoy them as you would any other green like kale or swiss chard.

Storing Kohlrabi: The leaves won't last as long as the bulb. So snip off the leaves and use within a day or so. Store the bulb wrapped in a bag or towel in the fridge. Don't peel until you're ready to use it. It will last 2 to 3 weeks in the fridge.

Preserving Kohlrabi: You can freeze it for future use in soups and stews, just peel, dice and blanch for 2 to 3 minutes and then submerge in ice water. Also, there are some great recipes out there for "fridge pickled" kohlrabi that look pretty easy. Here's one below:

Fridge Pickled Kohlrabi

This recipe makes one quart of pickles.
Ingredients:
4 small kohlrabi
2 large carrots
2 Tablespoons of salt
1 cup white vinegar
1 cup water
2 Tablespoons sugar
1 1/2 teaspoon of pickling or kosher salt
3 garlic cloves, roughly chopped
1 teaspoon of dill seeds
1/2 teaspoon of brown mustard seeds
6 black pepper corns, crushed

Directions: Start by peeling and slicing the kohlrabi. Place in a colander and salt with 2 T salt. Allow the kohlrabi to sit for an hour. In the meantime peel your carrots and cut into sticks. Combine all other ingredients in a sauce pan. When kohlrabi is done draining, rinse and pack with carrots into a quart jar. Boil remaining ingredients until all of the salt and sugar are dissolved and pour over carrots and kohlrabi. Cover and allow to cool on the counter then refrigerate. Let this sit in the fridge for two days before jumping in. Should be good in the fridge for 3 weeks.

Kohlrabi Slaw with Creamy Apple Dressing
Ingredients:
Dressing:
1/4 cup cream
1 Tablespoon fresh lemon juice
1/2 Tablespoon good mustard
1/2 teaspoon sugar
Salt & pepper to taste - go easy here
Fresh mint, chopped
Slaw:
1 pound fresh kohlrabi, trimmed, peeled, grated
2 apples, peeled, grated

Directions: Whisk cream into light pillows - this takes a minute or so, no need to get out a mixer. Stir in remaining dressing ingredients, the kohlrabi and apple. Serve immediately.

Kohlrabi Fritters:
makes 10 appetizer sized fritters
Ingredients:
1 small kohlrabi
1 medium yukon gold potato
1 Tablespoon of chives, thinly chopped
1 egg
3 Tablespoons of flour
1 Tablespoon of milk
Salt and pepper
Olive oil

Directions: Peel the kohlrabi and grate. Grate potato and mix with kohlrabi in. Add chives and egg and mix to combine. Add flour and milk to make a batter. Season with salt and pepper. Heat oil to medium heat in large skillet. Add the fritters, one heaping spoonful at a time. Flatten a little so the fritter is flat not round.

Fry each fritter for 4-5 minutes on each side. Turn when brown.. Drain on paper towel (this is when you want to salt them if you are going to again) and serve with sour cream or your favorite dipping sauce!

Roasted Garlic Kohlrabi

Ingredients:

1 1/2 pounds fresh kohlrabi, ends trimmed, thick green skin sliced off with a knife, diced1 Tablespoon olive oil2 Tablespoons of minced garlic

Chopped Chives

Grated parmesan

Salt and Pepper

Directions: Set oven to 450F. Toss the diced kohlrabi with olive oil, garlic and salt in a bowl. Spread evenly on a rimmed baking sheet and put into oven and roast for 30 - 35 minutes, stirring once. Sprinkle with chopped chives and grated parmesan.

Sautéed Kale and Kohlrabi

Adapted from Gourmet Magazine 2009

Ingredients:

1 1/4 pound kohlrabi, bulbs peeled

1/2 teaspoon grated lime zest

2 Tablespoons fresh lime juice

1/4 cup extra-virgin olive oil, divided

2 pounds kale (2 bunches), stems and center ribs discarded

5 garlic cloves, finely chopped

1/3 cup salted roasted pistachios, chopped

Directions: Very thinly slice kohlrabi with slicer. Whisk together lime zest and juice, 2 tablespoons oil, and 1/2 teaspoon each of salt and pepper in a large bowl. Toss kohlrabi with dressing.

Finely chop kale. Heat remaining 2 tablespoons oil in a 12-inch heavy skillet over medium-high heat until it shimmers. Sauté garlic until pale golden, about 30 seconds. Add kale by the handful, turning and stirring with tongs and adding more kale as volume in skillet reduces. When all of kale is wilted, sauté with 1/2 teaspoon salt until just tender, about 3 minutes. Transfer to a bowl and cool to room temperature. Toss kale with kohlrabi and pistachios.

L

Leeks

Leeks are one of my favorite vegetables because they are so versatile. They are part of the allium, (aka onion/garlic/scallions...) family. They have the most pleasant and mild onion flavor. I always find myself disappointed when the last leek is harvested and eaten so I dream of the days when they are in season again! Leeks are great as additions to soups, sauces, stir-fries, egg dishes, or eaten raw with a salad. Roasting leeks brings out their incredible sweet flavor too. When I'm making a soup I use leeks, carrots, celery AND onion. What a flavor! Leeks are great in stuffing too! You don't want to use the dark green parts, they are tough. Just the light green and white.

Storing Leeks: Leeks should be stored unwashed in the refrigerator, where they will keep fresh for between one and two weeks. Wrapping them loosely in a plastic bag will help them to retain moisture and keep the oniony smell from infiltrating other items in your fridge. If space is at a premium, you can chop off the dark green stem part before storing them.

Preserving Leeks: Leeks may be frozen after being blanched for two to three minutes, although they will lose some of their desirable taste and texture qualities. Leeks will keep in the freezer for about three months. I've dehydrated leeks in the past and used in the crockpot or added to soups or stir-fries in the winter. Also check out the confit recipe in the next few pages.

Roasted Leeks

Feel free to use a different spice combo rather than Herbs de Provence. I really like thyme or dill with leeks too!

Ingredients:

3 medium leeks, cleaned and cut lengthwise into quarters

1 Tablespoon of olive oil

1/2 teaspoon of Herbs de Provence

salt and pepper, to taste

Directions: Preheat oven to 400 degrees. Chop off the leek root ends and leafy dark green ends (light green is still good!) Cut the leeks in half lengthwise, rinse thoroughly, and cut each half in half. The leek pieces will naturally fall apart, and that's fine.

Preheat the oven to 400 degrees. In a roasting pan, toss leeks with olive oil, 1/2 tsp Herbs de Provence, and salt and pepper, to taste.

Roast leeks for 30 minutes or until tender.

Potato, Leek and Fennel Soup

Ingredients:

1 clove of garlic, minced

2 Tablespoons of butter

2 cups sliced leeks (white and pale green parts only)

2 cups sliced fennel bulb, fronds reserved for garnish

14 ½ oz low-salt chicken broth

4 cups of red-skinned potatoes, peeled, cut into 1/2-inch pieces

Directions: Melt butter in heavy large pot over medium-high heat. Add leeks and fennel and sauté until leeks are translucent, about 7 minutes. Add garlic and cook for a minute or two. Add broth and potatoes and bring to boil. Reduce heat to medium-low. Simmer soup until potatoes are very tender, about 25 minutes. Working in batches, puree soup in blender. Return to same pot. Re-warm soup if necessary. Season with salt and pepper. Ladle soup into bowls; garnish with reserved fennel fronds and serve.

Risotto with Beet Greens and Leeks

Recipe adapted from Cooking Light March 2001
Ingredients:
5 cups chicken broth
1 Tablespoon olive oil
2 cups thinly sliced leek (about 2 large)
1 ½ cups Arborio rice*
¼ cup white wine
3 cups coarsely chopped beet greens
¼ cup grated Parmesan
1/8 teaspoon black pepper
6 lemon wedges

Directions: Bring broth to a simmer in a medium saucepan (do not boil). Keep warm over low heat.
Heat oil in a large saucepan over medium heat. Add leek, sauté 4 minute or until tender. Add rice; cook 1 minute, stirring constantly. Stir in wine cook 1 minute or until the liquid is nearly absorbed stirring constantly. Reduce heat to low; stir in greens. Add broth 1/2 cup at a time, stirring constantly until each portion of the broth is absorbed before adding the next portion (about 25 minutes). Stir in cheese and pepper. Serve with lemon wedges.

*You may think you can substitute other types of rice for Arborio but you really can't in risotto dishes. Other medium-grain rice will give you the same creaminess but not the same al-dente bite that you get from Arborio rice. Luckily the availability of Arborio has increased in recent years so hit the rice or grain section of your local grocery and see what you can find!

Turnip or Rutabaga Puree with Leeks

from Deborah Madison's Vegetarian Cooking for Everyone
Ingredients:
1 small potato, peeled
2 pounds turnips and/or rutabagas, thickly peeled
2 medium chopped leeks, white and light green parts only
1 garlic clove or 1 stalk green garlic, chopped
salt and pepper
2 Tablespoons or more cream, buttermilk, or milk
2 Tablespoons of butter
2 teaspoon of chopped thyme

Directions: Chop the potato and turnips the same size. If using rutabagas, chop them about half the size of the potato. Put the vegetables, leeks, and garlic in a pot with cold water just to cover, add ½ t salt, and simmer, partially covered, until tender, 15-20 minutes. Drain, reserving the liquid. Mash the vegetables with a fork for a rough-textured puree or pass them through a food mill. Add 2 T or more cream or reserved broth to thin the puree. Stir in the butter and thyme and season with salt and pepper to taste.

Roasted Leek Confit

Adapted from The Glass Pantry
Ingredients:
2 lbs leeks (1 and 1/4 lb trimmed), sliced in half lengthwise, washed well, and sliced to 1/4-inch
6 Tablespoons of butter, melted (or about 1/3 cup olive oil)
1 teaspoon of salt
1/2 teaspoon of ground black pepper

Directions: Preheat oven to 350 degrees F. Arrange sliced leeks in a 9" x 13" shallow baking pan. Drizzle melted butter over leeks, add salt and pepper, and toss to evenly coat. Roast leeks, stirring every 15 minutes, until golden, about 1 to 1 and 1/2 hours. Add more butter (or oil) if leeks begin to dry out and brown. Essentially, they are done as soon as they taste good to you; I roast mine for a long time and let them get slightly brown, but you can stop at 45 minutes or so when they are still golden and very soft. Transfer to a clean pint jar to store. Serve warm or room temperature. Store in the fridge for up to two weeks.

Confit Options:
Toss with warm whole wheat pasta and a grating of parmesan or other hard cheese for a quick lunch.
Spread on top of whole wheat pizza crust with a little olive oil, basil, mozzarella and parmesan for a fantastic pizza.
Add to a warm turkey sandwich, or make a wrap with hummus and fresh parsley.
Dollop onto potato leek soup or stir into sour cream or yogurt for an onion-style dip.

Lettuce

To be perfectly honest most folks know how they like their lettuce. Romaine, salad mix, Bibb lettuce. They all are destined to be a salad right? Don't be so sure! We grow a lot of lettuce and we do so because we're good at it! We grow the right varieties in the summer to limit the bitterness the summer heat can sometimes bring. If you're in a CSA you'll notice that lettuce, of some type, is a frequent player. Don't get caught up thinking you have to eat the same old salad each time. Try something new!

Storing Lettuce: Wrap in a moist towel and/or put in a bag and store in your fridge's crisper drawer. Our salad mix lasts at least a week and romaine can last even longer.

Preserving Lettuce: Lettuce has a very high water content. Therefore it's nearly impossible to preserve lettuce for future use. Freezing it will make it mushy. Your best bet is to preserve it well and enjoy it fresh!

Ideas for lettuce that does not involve a salad:
Lettuce wraps (see recipe below)
Adding to sandwiches or pitas
Add to a smoothie (see recipe below)
Throw into your tomato sauce for extra nutrients

Green Lettuce Smoothie:
will make 2-3 smoothies
Ingredients:
1 cup of strawberries (between 12-16 strawberries)
2 large bananas
1/2 a head of romaine lettuce
2 cups water
Teaspoon of honey

Directions: wash berries and lettuce. Blend everything together.

Peach, Orange & Romaine Smoothie
Ingredients:
2 oranges, peeled and chopped
1 peach, pitted and chopped (skin left on but wash it first!)
4 to 6 large romaine leaves
1 cup of ice

Directions: Add everything to a blender and puree.

Wilted Lettuce Salad

A farmhouse favorite!

Ingredients:

5 slices bacon

2 Tablespoons red wine vinegar

1 Tablespoon lemon juice

1 teaspoon white sugar

1/2 teaspoon ground black pepper

1 head leaf lettuce, rinsed, dried and torn into bite-size pieces

6 green onions with tops, thinly sliced

Directions: Place bacon in a large, deep skillet. Cook over medium high heat until evenly brown. Remove from skillet, crumble and set aside.

To the hot bacon drippings, add the vinegar, lemon juice, sugar and pepper. Stir over medium heat until hot. In a large bowl, combine the lettuce and green onions. Add the warm dressing and toss to evenly coat. Sprinkle with bacon and serve.

Creamy Lettuce Soup

This is SO delicious!! Not something you hear of every day but something you'll make more than once! If you like bacon consider adding crumbled cooked bacon to the soup at the end!

Ingredients:
3 Tablespoons of butter
1 medium yellow onion, diced
4 – 6 garlic scapes coarsely chopped OR 2 garlic cloves, peeled
2 Tablespoons of coarsely chopped flat-leaf parsley
2 Tablespoons of coarsely chopped chives
1 Tablespoon of fresh thyme leaves
2 large heads of lettuce, ends trimmed and coarsely chopped
2 medium red potatoes, peeled and diced
3 cups chicken stock, homemade or low-sodium
1/4 cup heavy cream, plus extra for garnish
1/2 teaspoon of salt
1/4 teaspoon of ground black pepper

Directions: In a medium Dutch oven or soup pot, heat butter over medium. Add onion, and garlic scapes (or garlic) sauté over medium-low heat until vegetables are softened, about 5 minutes. Add parsley, chives and thyme; sauté for 1 minute. Add lettuce, stir and sauté until wilted, about 1 – 2 minutes. Add potatoes and stock; cover and bring to a boil. Reduce heat to maintain a simmer and cook, covered, until the potatoes are very tender, about 10 – 15 minutes. Process the soup with an immersion blender or transfer in batches to a blender or food processor. Add cream, salt & pepper: taste and adjust seasonings. Simmer for another 5 minutes or so, to heat through and reduce to desired thickness. Serve hot, garnished with a swirl of cream, scattered thyme leaves and fresh chives.

Grilled Romaine Hearts

Kind of a salad... but not really.

My Dad told me about this... he had it at a dinner party and the host grilled the romaine and then threw it in a pasta salad! I never would have thought of putting in a pasta salad but it sounds great! If you don't want to go the pasta salad route just grill these up as a side dish!

Ingredients:

2 Tablespoons extra virgin olive oil
1 Tablespoon lemon juice
1 small garlic clove , minced
1/2 teaspoon Dijon mustard
1/8 teaspoon Worcestershire sauce
1/4 teaspoon black pepper
2 Tablespoons grated parmesan cheese
2 romaine lettuce hearts
Olive oil for the grill

Directions: In a small bowl, whisk together the oil, lemon juice, garlic, mustard, Worcestershire and pepper. Stir in the Parmesan Cheese. Preheat the grill over medium-high heat, oil grill surface. Cut romaine in half length-wise and leave end intact so each half holds together. Grill until grill marks form and the lettuce wilts slightly, about 6 minutes. Turn once or twice. Drizzle with vinaigrette.

Asian Chicken Lettuce Wraps

Adapted from localkitchenblog.com

Ingredients:

Sauce:

1/4 cup brown sugar

1/4 cup soy sauce

1 teaspoon of rice vinegar

Chicken Stir-Fry:

3 Tablespoons of sesame oil

1 and 1/2 lbs chicken breast, diced to 1/2-inch strips

ground black pepper

2 stalks celery, trimmed and thinly sliced on the bias

2 medium carrots, peeled, trimmed and diced

4 green onions, diced

½ medium onion, diced

1 small head bok choi, chopped

3 large cloves garlic, minced

For serving:

1 to 2 heads large leaf lettuce

Directions: In a small bowl, whisk together brown sugar, soy sauce and vinegar and whisk until combined. Set aside. In a wok or large skillet, heat oil over high heat until shimmering. Add chicken and stir-fry over high heat until just cooked through, about 3 – 4 minutes. Add freshly ground black pepper to taste. Transfer chicken to a clean plate.

Add celery, carrots, onion, bok choi and garlic to hot oil in the wok or skillet and stir-fry over medium-high heat until just softened, about 1 – 2 minutes. Return the chicken to the wok, add the sauce and cook, stirring, for about 1 – 2 minutes, until chicken is heated through. Transfer to a serving bowl.

Spoon a small amount of chicken stir-fry, with sauce, into the center of a lettuce leaf. Add hot sauce if desired. Roll and eat like a burrito!

M

Mustard Greens

Mustard greens are the leaves from the mustard plant. If the plant was left to flower, the seeds would be what are used to make Dijon mustard. However these leaves don't taste anything like Dijon mustard! They have a peppery taste that will kick up the volume on whatever you're eating. Packed full of vitamins like K, A and C, you'll want to include these in your diet to get the excellent antioxidant properties and are good for your heart!! You can use mustard greens in many ways! Try throwing them in any soup or in the crockpot with your roast. You can eat them raw in a salad or on a sandwich or sauté them for a nice side dish or in a stir fry. The peppery, spicy kick that you get from raw mustard greens completely disappears once they are cooked.

Storing Mustard Greens: Place in a bag, unwashed, and store in the fridge for up to 4 or 5 days.

Preserving Mustard Greens: Freezing is one option for preserving your greens. It's nice in the winter to just grab a bag of blanched greens and use in soups, or any recipe that calls for cooked greens (i.e. not salads!). When freezing, just use the regular blanching method (wash greens, submerge in boiling water for 1 ½ minutes, remove, drain and pack into freezer bags). In some parts of China mustard greens are preserved with salt and added to dishes like stir-fries. I've also included an easy and flavorful way to make pickled mustard greens!

Sautéed Mustard Greens

Ingredients:

6 cups loosely packed mustard greens, chopped

3-4 cloves of garlic, crushed

½ medium red onion, sliced into rings

1 Tablespoon of olive oil

¼ cup vegetable stock or water

2 Tablespoon white vinegar

1 Tablespoon crushed red pepper

salt to taste

Directions: Heat oil in a pan, add the garlic and layer the onions, sprinkle some salt. Add the greens, stock and vinegar. Cover and cook on medium low heat for about 15-20 minutes, checking to make sure there is enough liquid, until greens are cooked to your liking Serve warm with plain rice or just plain!

Grapefruit, Mustard Green and Date Salad

CSA member Jennifer Swartout (adapted from Epicurious)

Ingredients:

1 Tablespoon finely chopped shallot

1 Tablespoon fresh lime juice

1 1/2 Tablespoons olive oil

¼ teaspoon sugar

¼ teaspoon salt

1 small pink or red grapefruit

¼ lb young mustard greens, trimmed and cut into 1/2-inch pieces (2 cups)

¼ cup dried dates, pitted and chopped

Directions: Stir together shallot and lime juice in a small bowl and let stand 5 minutes. Whisk in oil, sugar, and salt. Cut and peel any white pith from grapefruit with a sharp knife, then cut sections free from membranes. Toss mustard greens with dates in a large bowl.

Just before serving, toss greens with dressing and salt to taste. Divide salad between 2 plates and top with grapefruit sections.

Pickled Mustard Greens

Ingredients:

2 Tablespoons of sugar

1 Tablespoons of salt

1/4 cup white vinegar

1/2 lb. mustard greens

3 red or green serrano chiles, split lengthwise

Directions: In a small saucepan, combine 2 cups water, sugar, salt, and vinegar. Bring to a boil over high heat, then remove from heat. Cool slightly.

Using a paring knife, trim stems of washed mustard greens from leaves. Cut stems into 2" pieces and place in a 1-quart measuring cup. Coarsely chop enough greens to fill the measuring cup when added to stems and packed down gently.

Pack stems, leaves, and chiles into a clean glass 1-quart jar. Pour hot liquid onto greens, making sure that the stems are completely submerged. Cover and refrigerate for at least 3 days before serving.

Makes 1 quart

Penne Pasta with Bacon and Mustard Greens

Ingredients:

1 lb. box of penne pasta
1/2 lb. bacon, cut in 1/2-inch pieces
2 cups of mustard green leaves
2 Tablespoons of tomato paste
1 onion, chopped fine
3 cloves garlic, minced.
1/4 cup chicken stock
1 teaspoon of Italian Seasoning
1/4 teaspoon of crushed red pepper flakes
1 Tablespoon of extra virgin olive oil
Freshly grated Parmesan cheese to taste
Salt and pepper to taste.

Directions: Cook Penne according to package directions. Drain well but do not rinse.

Cook bacon in a large skillet over medium low heat until it is cooked through, but not crispy. Remove from grease and place on paper towels to drain.

Add olive oil to the same skillet (discard most bacon fat but leave a little for taste). Add onion and garlic, stirring until onion is translucent and garlic is fragrant. Add tomato paste and stir through. Toss in mustard greens and sauté until wilted. Return bacon to pan and toss well. Add Italian seasoning, red pepper flakes, chicken stock, salt and pepper. Taste for seasoning.

Add pasta and toss to coat well. Grate approximately 1/4 cup Parmesan cheese over pasta, toss well. Serve hot with additional Parmesan on top if desired.

Southern Pesto

A spin on the traditional basil pesto! Great on top of meat or fish, mixed in with pasta or added to scrambled eggs!
Ingredients:
1 pound of mustard greens
1 1/2 oz parmesan cheese
3 small garlic cloves, chopped
1/4 cup + 1 tablespoon olive oil
 1/2 teaspoon of salt & 1/4 teaspoon of pepper)
dash cayenne (optional)

Directions: In a big pot, filled halfway with water, bring to a boil. Place mustard greens in boiling water & cook for 2 minutes, drain & pat dry with a paper towel. Place mustard greens, cheese & garlic in a food processor and pulse until it appears loosely chopped. Slowly add your olive oil & continue pulsing until it forms a nice thick sauce. Season with salt & pepper to taste.

O

Okra

Our okra plants produce these huge beautiful flowers right before it sets the fruit (or the part of the plant we know as okra). It is a member of the hibiscus family after all! I am so tempted to pick those flowers but have to stop myself because without the flowers there's no okra! Sometimes I question whether the flowers are more valuable than the okra itself! I've had the mushy okra that people speak of. It's not worth sacrificing the huge, gorgeous flower! However there are recipes out there that I have prepared that make me ignore that flower and keep wishing for more okra! Truth is okra can be really tasty when prepared correctly.

Storing Okra: Wet pods will quickly mold, so don't wash before storing. Just place in a brown paper bag and store in the refrigerator immediately after getting home.

Preserving Okra: When I think of preserving okra, I think of pickled okra! You can also freeze it. Here's how: Wash the pods and cut of the stems. Submerge in a boiling pot of water for 3 minutes (smaller pods) or 4 minutes (larger pods). Remove and dunk in ice water until cool. Drain. You can bag them whole or if you plan on using your frozen okra for frying later you can go ahead and slice them and coat in your flour/cornmeal/seasoning mix. Place in a plastic freezer bag and you're good to go!

Pickled Okra
Makes three pints
Ingredients:
1 ½ to 2 pounds tender okra pods
3 cloves garlic, peeled
3 teaspoon canning salt
3 teaspoon dill seed (or 9 heads of fresh dill)
3/4 teaspoon of whole peppercorns1
1/2 cups white vinegar
1 ½ cups water

Directions: Wash the okra in cold water. Trim the stems. Peel the garlic, but leave it whole. Into the sterile jars, pack as many pods of okra as possible with the tips pointing up. To each jar add 1 teaspoon of canning salt, 1 whole garlic clove, 1 teaspoon of dill seed and 1/4 teaspoon of whole peppercorns. Bring the vinegar and water to a boil. Fill jars with the vinegar and water mixture to within 1/4 inch of the rim. Place the lids and rings on the jars and process in a boiling water bath for 10 minutes. Let cool and store in a cool, dark place. (If you're canning, please become familiar with the process of canning. Ball's Blue Book is an excellent resource. You can also place the jars in the fridge rather than processing in a hot water bath and they should last a few months).

Southern Fried Okra
This is the standard but in a non-slimy way!
Ingredients:
10-12 large pods of okra (or double the number of small)
1 egg
cornmeal
salt and pepper
1 teaspoon of chili powder
oil for frying

Directions: Wash the okra and slice them into approximately 1.5cm chunks. Beat the egg and dump all the okra pieces into the bowl with it. Stir well so that each okra piece is coated well.

In another bowl, add some cornmeal and season it well with salt, pepper and chili powder. Use a fork to transfer the okra lumps to the cornmeal (you just want enough egg to hold that cornmeal on). Coat each lump well and set aside – they're ready for frying. Heat some oil for deep frying – it should be ready when a piece of okra sizzles happily in there. Fry in small batches, turning occasionally, until they are golden brown. Drain on kitchen paper and serve warm. Serves 1-2 as a side or snack.

Chicken Gumbo

I've been to New Orleans twice in my lifetime and have always dreamed of living there. The people, the music, the FOOD! Try this Creole dish and you won't be disappointed. It makes a lot and is great to freeze leftovers.

Ingredients:

1 broiler/fryer chicken (3-4 pounds), cut up
2 quarts water
1/4 cup canola oil or bacon drippings
2 Tablespoons all-purpose flour
2 medium onions, chopped
2 celery ribs, chopped
1 medium green pepper, chopped
3 garlic cloves, minced
1 can (28 ounces) tomatoes, drained (or 6 chopped fresh tomatoes)
2 cups fresh or frozen sliced okra
2 bay leaves
1 teaspoon dried basil
1 teaspoon salt
1/2 teaspoon pepper
1 to 2 teaspoons hot pepper sauce
2 Tablespoons sliced green onions
Hot cooked rice

Directions: Place chicken and water in a large pot or dutch oven. Cover and bring to a boil. Reduce heat; cover and simmer for 30-45 minutes or until chicken is tender. Remove chicken and reserve broth for later use. Set chicken aside until cool enough to handle without burning yourself. Remove chicken from bones; discard bones and cut into meat into cubes; set aside.

In a large stock pot, combine oil or drippings and flour until smooth. Cook over medium-high heat for 3 minutes, stirring constantly. Reduce heat to medium. Cook and stir about 3 minutes more or until mixture is reddish, copper-brown. Don't leave the stove while you're doing this. You can go from a perfect roux to a burnt disaster in a few seconds. Just keep stirring! Turn the heat to high. Stir in 2 cups reserved broth. Bring to a boil; cook and stir for 2 minutes or until thick.

Add the onions, celery, and green pepper; cook and stir for 5 minutes. Add garlic and cook another minute. Add the tomatoes, okra, bay leaves, basil, salt, pepper and pepper sauce. Cover and simmer for 1-1/2 to 2 hours.

Remove and throw away bay leaves. Garnish with green onions. Serve with rice.

Roasted Okra

A quick and simple recipe that keeps the slime at bay!

Ingredients:

18 fresh okra pods, sliced 1/3 inch thick

1 Tablespoon olive oil

2 teaspoons kosher salt, or to taste

1 teaspoon black pepper, or to taste

Directions: Preheat an oven to 425 degrees F. Arrange the okra slices in one layer on a foil lined cookie sheet. Drizzle with olive oil and sprinkle with salt and pepper. Bake in the preheated oven for 10 to 15 minutes.

Vegan Gumbo

Ingredients:

3 Tablespoons olive oil

1/4 cup flour

1 medium sized onion, diced large

3 cloves garlic, minced

1 heaping cup sweet red peppers, diced large (or one red bell pepper)

2 cups chopped tomatoes

1 teaspoon salt

Fresh black pepper

2 bay leaves

2 teaspoons smoked paprika

A couple dashes of hot sauce

8 springs fresh thyme (plus extra for garnish)

2 1/2 to 3 cups vegetable broth at room temperature

2 cups okra, sliced 1/4 inch thick or so

1 1/2 cups cooked kidney beans (a 15 oz can, rinsed and drained)

1 1/2 cup cooked garbanzo beans (a 15 oz can, rinsed and drained)

1 Tablespoon fresh lemon juice

Directions: To make the roux: Preheat a large, heavy bottom pot over medium-low heat. Add the oil and sprinkle in the flour. Use a wooden spoon to gently toss the flour in the oil, and stir pretty consistently for 3 to 4 minutes, until the flour is turns a copper colored brown. Turn the up temp to high and add the vegetable broth slowly and stir constantly until thickened.

Add the onion, peppers and tomatoes and cook down for about 10 more minutes. Season with fresh black pepper, salt, bay leaves, smoked paprika and thyme and mix well. Add the okra and beans and chickpeas and hot sauce. Turn the heat up and cover to bring to a boil. Stir occasionally.

Once boiling, reduce the heat to a simmer and let cook uncovered for 30 to 45 minutes, stirring occasionally, until the stew is nicely thickened and the okra is tender. If it's too thick, thin with up to 1/2 cup vegetable broth. If it's not as thick as you like, just cook it a bit longer.

Add the lemon juice, and adjust salt and pepper to your liking. Let it sit for 10 minutes. Remove bay leaves and thyme stems (if you can see them) then serve in a bowl with rice.

Onions

"It's hard to imagine civilization without onions." -Julia Child

In my house there is almost always an onion or two. I put onions in every savory dish I can. One of my favorite "smells" is mirepoix (the classic celery, carrots and onion combo used in soups and stocks). I've watched in envy as Julia Child chopped onions like no other. My favorite soup of all time is French Onion. However, as much as I love eating and cooking with onions I do not find pleasure growing them! It's really just a personal thing. Onions aren't hard to grow. But it seems like every time we've grown onions the conditions aren't ideal. For instance almost every time the ground is rock hard when we're planting them. So I'm on hands and knees (a classic organic farmer pose) for hours while clods of dirt were leaving deep impressions on my palms and legs. Then, like clockwork we get a ton of spring rain and can't get into the fields to weed before the get out of control. You could barely seed the onion plants through the weeds! Onions don't like to share their space with weeds one bit so you really have to weed constantly. Finally it would dry up enough so Hans, Dave and I spent hours and hours weeding those onions plants by hand. I cursed every single one of those weeds. Apparently I wasn't very convincing because more grew back in their place. When it comes to harvesting onions, truthfully... it's not too bad. Except one time I was driving the garden fork into the ground when I hit a snake. I accidentally pierced right through it, dropped the fork and ran screaming. Oops.

Storing onions: Onions will last for quite awhile if stored in a dark, cool place. The garage or basement are great places. Also, if an onion feels a little soft on the outside you don't have to throw it away. Usually, it's just a couple of the outside layers and once peeled away, the rest of the onion is perfect!

Preserving onions: If stored correctly, onions should last a pretty long time. However, a great way to preserve onions for later use is to caramelize them when you have the time and freeze them. I use my own frozen caramelized onions in my French Onion soup (see recipe) and in quiches, tossed with sautéed green beans, on top of burgers or mashed potatoes or really in just about any dish you can think of. They are pretty tasty even on their own. Here's how:

Katie' Caramelized Onions:
Peel 3-4 onions and cut into slices. It doesn't really matter how thick they are. Heat about 2 tablespoons of butter over medium-high heat in a frying pan, and when the butter starts to foam, add the onions. Make sure and use butter (unless you don't want to use butter...) but margarine just isn't the same thing.. Turn the heat to medium and cook, stirring frequently.

As the onions cook they will gradually begin to turn golden, then a deep brown. As they do, keep a watchful eye on them - you don't want them to actually burn.* Let them cook for about 20 minutes, stirring often and turning the heat down if they're beginning to burn. When they are a deep brown, take them off the heat. Let cool and then freeze in ice cube trays or a muffin pan. Once frozen, pop out and store in freezer bags

***An important note**: Burnt onions and caramelized onions are NOT the same thing. There's no reason to turn your heat to high, all guns blazing, trying to COOK those onions in a minute flat. It's all about the slow sauté. The browning is from the sugars slowly turning brown due to the temperature exceeding 300 degrees. This is caramelizing. Burning your onions at high temps because you aren't being patient enough is just burnt onions. Ick. Slow down, enjoy the aroma of the onions, listen to the subtle sizzling and get lost in the simple task of stirring.

Onion Pie
Grandma Betty Micetic
Ingredients:
4 cups of thinly sliced sweet onions
3 Tablespoons of melted butter
1 1/2 cups of sour cream
2 eggs - well beaten
1/2 cup of milk
3 Tablespoons of flour
1 teaspoon of salt
1 partially baked pie shell
Bacon, cooked and crisp

Directions: Sauté onions in butter until lightly browned. Whisk together sour cream, eggs and milk, Add onions. In a separate bowl mix the flour and salt. Combine with the onion mixture. Pour into pie crust and bake at 325 degrees for 45-60 minutes. Garnish with crumbled bacon.

Pickled Red Onions

We add ours to tacos, salads, on top of burgers or sandwiches. We just love these things and they last forever in the refrigerator! You'll be very surprised when the liquid turns a BRIGHT pinkish color. It's actually pretty amazing that the red skin of the onion can so drastically change the color in such a short amount of time.

Ingredients:

1 red onion

½ cup of apple cider vinegar

1 Tablespoon of sugar or honey

1 ½ teaspoon of salt

1 bay leaf

1 cup of water

Directions: Thinly slice the red onion. In a saucepan whisk together vinegar, water salt and sugar/honey. Heat until sugar is dissolved. Put sliced onions in a quart sized mason jar and pour hot liquid over the onions. Add a bay leaf and seal. Allow to cool and then store in refrigerator. At least allow to cool before eating them!

French Onion Soup

I've tried every version I can find. Although my favorite is from a restaurant in Lincoln, Illinois (I think I need to get to France ASAP!) this is a close second! This recipe calls for wine and it really does make a big difference in taste (Don't worry the alcohol burns off). If you caramelize the onions ahead of time and freeze them this soup cooks up quick.

Ingredients:

4 Tablespoons (1/2 stick) unsalted butter

3 Tablespoons olive oil

3 lb. yellow onions, thinly sliced

1/2 teaspoons of salt

1 1/2 Tablespoon all-purpose flour

2 quarts beef stock

1/2 cup dry white wine

1 teaspoon of freshly ground pepper

2 sprigs of thyme, removed when soup is served

6 to 8 slices of french bread

1/2 lb. shredded cheese like gruyère , provolone or mozzarella cheese

Directions: First you need to caramelize your onions. See the directions for Katie's Caramelized Onions at the beginning of this section. Just use the 4 Tablespoons of butter and 3 pounds of onions.

In a saucepan, bring the beef stock and wine to a boil over high heat. Slowly add the stock mixture to the onions, stirring to blend. Add the salt, pepper and thyme. Reduce the heat to medium, cover partially and simmer about 45 minutes.

Meanwhile, place the bread on a baking sheet, drizzle with olive oil and toast under the broiler, turning once, until golden, 3 to 4 minutes per side. You can also just bake in an 400 degree oven until toasty and brown. Pour soup into bowls, place your crispy bread slice on the surface of the soup and sprinkle your cheese on top. You can ladle the soup into oven-safe bowls and stick them in a 400 degree oven until the cheese is brown and melted. Or if you're like me and you just can't wait, you can skip that step!

Caramelized Onion and Goat Cheese Cornbread
Adapted from Smitten Kitchen.com
Ingredients:
1 cup of cornmeal
2 cups of buttermilk
1 to 2 Tablespoons oil or butter
2 cups of onions, diced
3/4 cups unbleached, all-purpose flour
1 1/2 Tablespoons baking powder
1/4 teaspoon baking soda
1 teaspoon salt
6 ounces of goat cheese
2 Tablespoons honey
1/4 cup granulated sugar
3 large eggs, at room temperature
2 Tablespoons unsalted butter, melted
2 1/2 cups fresh or frozen corn kernels
2 Tablespoons bacon fat, vegetable oil or butter

Directions: Preheat the oven to 350°F. Heat a large sauté pan to medium and coat the bottom with 1 to 2 tablespoons of butter or oil. Add the onions and cook them until they're well-caramelized with browned edges. Season with salt and set aside (See Katie's Caramelized Onions recipe for more info on caramelized onions).

Sift together the flour, baking powder, baking soda and salt and set aside.
Using a mixer or beater, beat the goat cheese on medium until fluffy. Add the eggs, one at a time and scraping down

the bowl between each. (If it looks like it's going to curd, don't worry. It's fine.) Add the melted butter, honey, sugar, cornmeal and buttermilk and mix until smooth. Add the flour mixture and stir until combined and then gently stir in the corn kernels, mixing them until the ingredients are incorporated.

Place two tablespoons of bacon fat, vegetable oil or butter in a 10 inch round cake pan (you can also use a cast-iron skillet, 9 by 13-inch baking pan or a 12-inch square pan). Place the pan in the oven for 5 to 7 minutes, until the fat gets very hot. With good pot holders, remove the pan and tilt it to grease the corners and sides. Pour in the batter, spreading it evenly and sprinkle the caramelized onion evenly over the top.

Bake for about 30 minutes, or until the cornbread is firm and springing (the baking time will depend on the size and type of pan) and a toothpick inserted into the center comes out clean. Serve immediately.

P

Pak Choi /Bok Choy

Is it Bok Choy or Pak Choi? Or Pok Choi? They are all basically the same name for a vegetable known as Chinese cabbage (Napa Cabbage is also a form of Chinese cabbage). Even though they are known as Chinese cabbage, they don't have the cabbage flavor you'd think of with traditional western cabbage. The crunchy stalks resemble celery and I've even used them to replace raw celery in a veggie tray or pasta salad. The leaves have a crisp flavor that can be used in a variety of dishes. I love chopping it up with cilantro and using in place of lettuce when I make tacos. However most recipes out there use bok choy in soups and stir fries. If you see any calling for either Bok Choy or Pak Choi you can use either. They are interchangeable.

Storing Bok Choi/Pak Choi : Wrap unwashed in a damp towel or in a bag in your crisper drawer. They should last 3-5 days.

Preserving Bok Choi/Pak Choi: You can freeze Bok Choy leaves by blanching them but freezing the stems can result in mush. It's not uncommon to see clotheslines filled with drying bok choy in small Chinese villages (however our climate isn't very hospitable to drying it outdoors). Dried bok choy can be reconstituted in soups and stews and has a more intense flavor. There are recipes out there specifically called "Dried Bok Choy Soup."

Here's how to do it with your stove, but you can also use a food dehydrator: Wash and dry the bok choy thoroughly. Fill the 2-qt. pot three-quarters full of water and bring to a boil over high heat. Fill a bowl 3/4's of the way with ice and water. Cut the bok choy into quarters, lengthwise, leaving a portion of the root in each of the quarters to prevent the bok choy from falling apart. Place the bok choy into the water once it reaches a rolling boil. Boil for two minutes and immediately remove the bok choy to the bowl of ice water to stop the cooking process. Pull out the bok choy and set aside on a towel to drain. Repeat with the remaining bok choy until all of the vegetables have been blanched. Pat the bok choy dry. Lay the bok choy onto a baking sheet in a single layer. Place in an oven at 200 degrees with the oven door slightly ajar for eight to 12 hours or until the bok choy have dried. Turn the bok choy every two hours to ensure even drying. Store in an air tight container until ready to use.

Chicken Adobo Soup with Bok Choy

A Pilipino soup that's super easy to make!

Ingredients

1/3 cup reduced-sodium soy sauce

1/3 cup rice vinegar

2 garlic cloves, sliced

1 bay leaf

1 teaspoon olive oil

1/2 yellow onion, chopped

4 cups chicken stock or broth

1 1/2 cups skinned and shredded roasted or boiled chicken breast meat

1/2 cup uncooked whole-wheat couscous or 1 cup cooked brown rice

1/2 pound baby bok choy, halved lengthwise & sliced crosswise 1/2-inch wide

2 green onions, including tender green tops, thinly sliced

Directions: In a small saucepan, combine the soy sauce, vinegar, garlic and bay leaf over medium-high heat. Heat the mixture until it just comes to a boil. Remove from the heat and set aside.

In a large saucepan, heat the olive oil over medium heat. Add the yellow onion and sauté until soft and lightly golden, about 6 minutes. Add the chicken stock and bring to a boil. Add the soy sauce mixture, chicken and couscous. Return to a boil, reduce the heat to medium, and simmer for 2 minutes. Add the bok choy and simmer until the bok choy is tender, about 2 minutes. Discard the bay leaf. Ladle into warmed individual bowls and garnish with the green onions.

Stir-Fried Rice

If you don't like mushrooms or have other veggies on hand feel free to substitute.

Ingredients:

2 1/4 cups water

1 1/2 cups long grain rice (or jasmine, or leftover rice... whatever you've got!)

2 1/2 Tablespoons of vegetable oil

4 eggs, beaten

3 carrots, thinly sliced

3 cups thinly sliced bok choy leaves and stems

1 cup of snow peas, sliced thin into slivers

1/4 lb. shitake mushrooms, stems removed and caps sliced

1 1/2 Tablespoons sesame oil

3 green onions sliced

Salt and pepper

Directions: Prepare rice as directed on box. Heat 1 1/2 tablespoons vegetable oil in wok or heavy large skillet over high heat until hot but not smoking. Scramble eggs like you'd normally do and set aside. Heat remaining 1 tablespoon vegetable oil in wok or large pan over high heat. Add slivered carrots and stir-fry 1 minute. Add sliced bok choy, sliced mushroom caps and slivered snow peas.

Sprinkle with salt and pepper and stir-fry until vegetables just begin to soften, about 4 minutes. Add oriental sesame oil and heat mixture, then add cooked rice and stir-fry until heated through. Stir in eggs and sliced green onions. Season rice to taste with salt and pepper and serve immediately.

Bok Choy Salad

Ingredients:

1/2 cup olive oil

1/4 cup white vinegar

1/3 cup of sugar

3 Tablespoons soy sauce

2 bunches baby bok choy, cleaned and sliced

1 bunch green onions, chopped

1/8 cup slivered almonds, toasted

1 cup of chow mein noodles (optional)

Directions: Wisk together olive oil, white vinegar, sugar, and soy sauce. Combine the bok choy, green onions, almonds, and chow mein noodles in a salad bowl. Toss with dressing, and serve.

Braised Bok Choy with Garlic & Ginger

Ingredients:

1 cup vegetable broth

1 Tablespoon unsalted butter

1 clove garlic, minced

1 1/2 teaspoons minced fresh ginger

1 pound bok choy, rinsed, drained, and sliced lengthwise

1 teaspoon sesame oil

Salt and ground black pepper

Directions: Bring broth, butter, garlic, and ginger to a simmer in a large heavy skillet. Arrange bok choy stems and stalk evenly in skillet, cover, and simmer until tender, about 5 minutes. Add green leafy parts, and cook 3 minutes more. Stir occasionally. Using tongs, transfer bok choy to a serving dish, cover, and keep warm.Bring the liquid to a boil and simmer until reduced to about 1/4 cup. Stir in toasted sesame oil and pour mixture over bok choy. Season with sea salt and pepper, if desired.

Parsley Root

It's a parsnip. It's a Carrot. No its parsley root! Parsley root looks like a parsnip or a white carrot. But it's a vegetable that stands all on its own. It has a wonderful, aromatic flavor with hints of carrots, celeriac, turnips and yep you guessed it... parsley. You can use it just like you would any other root crop. Roast it to bring out its sweetness. Toss it in the crock pot with your roast or chicken. Mash it or sauté it. Add it to soups. The possibilities are endless! Properties in the parsley root have been known to aid with liver and gallbladder issues and it's a wonderful blood purifier!

Storing Parsley Root: Parsley root will keep in the refrigerator for up to 2 weeks if you first wrap it in a damp paper towel and place it in a plastic bag. It's best to cut the green tops off if you don't plan on using the parsley root soon. You can use the tops like regular parsley.

Preserving Parsley Root: You can freeze parsley root just like most other roots. Wash and peel the root, dice into 1 inch cubes and blanch for 2 minutes. Remove and submerge into ice water. Drain and package into freezer bags. Frozen parsley root is great for soups later in the colder months!

Parsley Root Fries
Ingredients:
3 parsley roots – about 1.5 lbs
Olive Oil
Salt
freshly ground black pepper
Fresh rosemary and thyme

Directions: Preheat oven to 400°F. Peel roots and cut them into french-fry sized sticks. The thinner, the crispier they will be. Toss with some oil, a few pinches of salt, pepper, and fresh rosemary and thyme.

Roast for 20 minutes, toss, and place back in the oven for another 5-10 minutes until golden on the edges.

Parsley Root And Parsnip Casserole
Ingredients:
3/4 pound parsnips
3/4 pound parsley root
1 pound russet, Yukon gold potatoes
1 clove garlic, crushed
salt and freshly ground pepper to taste
2 Tablespoons unsalted butter
1 to 1 1/2 cups heavy cream

Directions: Preheat the oven to 400 degrees. Peel the parsnips, parsley root and potatoes and slice them very thin (the slicing can be done with a food processor or a mandolin).

Lightly butter a glass baking dish and rub it with the crushed clove of garlic. Layer the vegetable slices in the dish, seasoning with salt and pepper as you go. Top with butter cut in small pieces and pour on just enough cream to moisten the vegetables.

Cover loosely with foil and bake for 15 minutes. Uncover and bake another 30 minutes or until the vegetables are tender. If they get too dry add more cream.

Kale and Parsley Root Soup

Ingredients:

1 bunch curly green kale leaves, separated from the stem

1 parsley root bulb, peeled and chopped

1 onion, diced

3 large carrots chopped into slices

1 large sweet potato, peeled and chopped into thick slices

32 oz of broth – either vegetable or low sodium chicken broth

1 Tablespoon of Olive oil

1 Tablespoon of butter

½ teaspoon of fresh thyme, chopped.

Salt & pepper

¾ cup of coconut milk (you can use half and half instead. It changes the flavor a bit but you still keep that creamy consistency.

1 cup coarsely chopped parsley (use the green tops of your parsley root)

Directions: Over medium-high heat a large pot or dutch oven on the stove add butter and olive oil. Add the parsley root, onion and carrots and toss until coated. Sprinkle with a large pinch of salt and thyme. Sauté vegetables until tender (about 5-7 minutes) Add the broth and bring to a boil.

Add the sweet potatoes and lower heat to medium. Simmer until potatoes are soft (6-7 minutes).

Stir in the kale leaves and turn off heat. Lastly, stir in the coconut milk and parsley.

Let the hot mixture sit a few minutes as you season to taste with salt and pepper. Ladle into bowls and garnish with fresh parsley.

Flatbread with Potatoes, Parsley Root and Fennel

Ingredients:

2 teaspoons olive oil

3 cloves garlic, sliced

4 1/2 cups diced potatoes

1 medium parsley root, diced

1 small fennel bulb, diced

1/2 cup water

1 teaspoon dried rosemary

1 teaspoon Hungarian paprika

salt and pepper to taste

4 slices of flatbread or wheat tortillas

Directions: Preheat a cast iron pan or another heavy bottom pan to high heat. Add oil, garlic, potatoes, parsley root, and fennel. Sauté for 1-2 minutes and reduce heat to medium. Add spices, stir, and add water. Cover with a lid and cook for 15-20 minutes until potatoes and parsley root are soft.

Place flatbreads on plates, fill with potato mixture, and sprinkle some cilantro on top. Serve immediately and add hot sauce if you like.

Parsnips

One of my all-time favorite vegetables! Sweeter than a carrot with an earthier flavor. They are packed full of potassium but lack the beta-carotene of its cousin the carrot. It has the starchy consistency of a potato so it can be used either to replace a potato when mashing or adding it into your mashed potato recipe for extra nutrients and a buttery flavor. Although it's my favorite vegetable it is also my nemesis. They are so terribly difficult for us to grow. Either we can't get the seed to germinate. Or when we do, it grows so much slower than the weeds around it and we can't keep up with hoeing or hand-weeding. Or, in the case of this recent spring, a cow or two got out of the pasture and trampled all over our beds of parsnips! My guess is that my love of parsnips has something to do with how obscure they are in my household!

Storing parsnips: Store in your crisper drawer for up to three weeks. Parsnips should be scrubbed rather than peeled.

Preserving parsnips: Wash and peel the root, dice into 1 inch cubes and blanch for 2 minutes. Remove and submerge into ice water. Drain and package into freezer bags. You can then later add them to soups or puree for a yummy mash! You can also pickle and can parsnips but the consistency isn't always ideal. If you are going to can parsnips make sure you use a pressure canner as they are a low acidic vegetable!

Parmesan Parsnip Mash

Ingredients:

1/2 pound parsnips, peeled and cut into chunks

½ pound of potatoes, peeled (russet, yukon gold, etc.)

4 cups cold water

1/2 teaspoon salt

1 Tablespoon extra virgin olive oil

1/4 cup plain Greek yogurt (you can also use sour cream)

1 Tablespoon of cream (I use half and half but you can also use heavy cream)

1/8 teaspoon coarse salt

Ground black pepper

1/4 cup freshly shredded Parmesan cheese

Directions: In a saucepan combine parsnips, potatoes, water and 1/2 teaspoon salt. Bring to boiling; reduce heat and simmer 20 to 25 minutes until parsnips and potatoes are very tender. Drain; return parsnips and potatoes to saucepan. Mash with a potato masher or fork. Stir in olive oil, yogurt, 1/8 teaspoon salt and pepper to taste. Stir in half of the Parmesan cheese. Sprinkle with remaining Parmesan cheese on top when serving. Note: You can use more potatoes and fewer parsnips or more parsnips and less potatoes. The choice is yours!

Pasta with Parsnips, Kale and Caramelized Onions:
Ingredients:
1 Tablespoon extra-virgin olive oil, divided
1 Tablespoon of butter
3 cups diagonally cut parsnip (about 1 pound)
2 1/2 cups sliced onion (about 1 large)
1 Tablespoon chopped fresh thyme
4 garlic cloves, chopped
1/2 cup dry white wine
8 cups chopped kale, center stem removed
1/2 cup vegetable broth
8 ounces uncooked penne pasta
1/2 cup shaved Parmesan cheese, divided
1/2 teaspoon salt
1/2 teaspoon ground black pepper

Directions: Heat ½ tablespoon of butter and ½ tablespoon of oil in a large pan over medium heat. Add parsnip to pan; cook 12 minutes or until tender, stirring occasionally. Place in a large bowl; keep warm.

Heat remaining butter and oill in pan over medium-low heat. Add onion to pan; cook 20 minutes or until tender and golden brown, stirring occasionally. Stir in thyme and garlic; cook 2 minutes, stirring occasionally. Add wine; cook 3 minutes or until liquid almost evaporates. Stir in kale and broth; cook, covered, 3 minutes or until kale is tender.

Cook pasta according to package directions, drain pasta in a sieve over a bowl, reserving 3/4 cup cooking liquid. Add drained pasta to kale mixture. Stir in parsnips, 1/2 cup reserved cooking liquid, 1/4 cup cheese, 1/2 teaspoon salt, and 1/2 teaspoon black pepper; cook for 1 minute or until thoroughly heated. Top with more cheese.

Parsnip and Butternut Squash Hashbrowns
Ingredients:
2 cups of shredded/grated parsnips
2 cups of shredded/grated butternut squash
1/3 cup of grated or minced onion
1/4 teaspoon of salt
1/2 teaspoon of garlic powder
2 Tablespoon of fat (You can use butter, oil, or lard)
1/4 cup stock (vegetable or chicken)

Directions: Peel and grate the parsnips and squash. I used the shredded attachment on my food processor to make short work of it, but there's no reason you couldn't use a regular box grater. Finely mince or shred the onion.
Mix the parsnips, squash, onion, salt, garlic powder, and stock in a large bowl.
Melt the fat of your choice in a large pan on medium high. Add the mixture and flatten out. Let cook 3-4 minutes before stirring each time. If it appears your parsnips and squash are too dry, drizzle a little more stock over but go easy because you don't want to turn them to mush.
Turn, flip, stir, etc., every couple of minutes until it reaches your desired crispness level. I like mine super crispy so I cooked it for around 20 minutes.
Optional: add in diced green peppers, green onions, ham, diced bacon, etc.

Balsamic Roasted Carrots and Parsnips:

If you already ate all your carrots you can just use parsnips. Or add in turnips or rutabagas!

Ingredients:

4 ounces of goat cheese (crumbled)

1/4 cup chopped fresh, flat-leaf parsley

1 teaspoon lemon zest

1/2 teaspoon dried crushed red pepper

4 Tablespoons olive oil, divided

1 1/2 pounds carrots

1 1/2 pounds parsnips

2 Tablespoons light brown sugar

3 Tablespoons balsamic vinegar

Directions: Preheat oven to 400°. Toss together first 4 ingredients and 1 Tbsp. olive oil in a small bowl. Set aside. Cut carrots and parsnip into thin strips. Whisk together brown sugar, balsamic vinegar, and remaining 3 Tbsp. olive oil in a large bowl. Toss with carrots and parsnips, and place on a lightly greased sheet pan. . Sprinkle with desired amount of salt and freshly ground pepper.

4. Bake at 400° for 40 to 45 minutes or until vegetables are tender and browned, stirring every 15 minutes. Remove from oven and gently toss with cheese, herb and lemon zest mixture.

Peas

We grow snap peas, English peas and snow peas because well... we like peas a lot. It's something we can plant early in the spring when we're dying to get into the fields. When deciding how to use peas, most folks usually just think of steamed peas rolling around their plate. Eh... forggggeet about it. There are so many other wonderful things to do with peas. Worse, when people think about peas what pops into their brains are the army-green, mushy versions that showed up on school cafeteria trays. No thanks. I'll take fresh peas please! Here's the difference between the three different kinds of peas:

Fresh **snap peas** come in a pod and are eaten whole, pod and all. They are sweet and plump.

Snow peas are the ones that have a flat pod. These are eaten whole. We like to toss them in pasta and stir fries.

English peas or "garden peas" are the kind that you shell and have cute, little, round peas. You don't want to eat these whole as the pods are very tough. English peas actually have more nutrients than snap or snow peas! Shelling English peas is not a chore. I repeat. It is not a chore. This is something our grandmothers used to do on the front porch while sharing stories. This is a way to disconnect from the stresses of the day and listen to the rhythm of the "snap" of pod and the "ping" of the peas as they hit the bottom on the bowl. It's a relaxing, simple pastime and your reward is fresh peas!

Storing peas: Make sure you place them in the refrigerator when you bring them home! The crisper drawer will do. Don't wash them until you're ready to use them. Peas are best eaten as soon as you get them or they start to lose their sweet flavor. If you're dealing with English peas (the peas are still in the pod) here's how to remove them from the pod: Before you remove the peas from the pod, rinse them briefly under running water. To easily shell them, snap off the top and bottom of the pod and then gently pull off the "thread" that lines the seam of most peapods. For those that do not have "threads," carefully cut through the seam, making sure not to cut into the peas. Gently open the pods to remove the peas, which do not need to be washed since they have been encased in the pod.

Preserving Peas: Personally, I have no interest in canned peas. The fresh taste is not preserved when canned and the color drastically changes. I prefer to freeze mine, although drying is also a possibility with a food dehydrator. Here's a great way to freeze peas so you can use them in winter soups or stews, in a homemade pot pie or just eaten with a little butter and ground pepper. You'll be blanching them, so get a pot of water boiling and also a bowl of ice water nearby. If you're using English peas you'll need to shell them first. Otherwise, blanch with the entire pod. Place peas in boiling water for 60 seconds. Remove from the boiling water with a slotted spoon and quickly submerge into your bowl of ice water. Let sit for another minute. Drain and then place into a freezer bag and pop them in your freezer. Done!

Creamy Pasta with Peas

Ingredients:
salt and pepper
12 ounces farfalle pasta
1 ½ cups of shelled English peas
3/4 cup heavy cream
1/3 cup canned reduced-sodium chicken broth
1/2 cup grated Parmesan cheese
2 Tablespoons pine nuts
1 bunch arugula, tough stems removed, chopped

Directions: In a large pot of boiling salted water, cook pasta until al dente, according to package instructions; add peas 1 minute before end of cooking. Drain; return pasta and peas to pot. Next, in a large skillet, combine cream and chicken broth; simmer until thickened slightly, 7 minutes. Stir in Parmesan until melted. Add sauce to pasta and peas; toss to combine. Season with salt. Toast pine nuts in a skillet over medium heat, shaking frequently, until golden, 1 to 2 minutes. Add to pasta along with arugula; season with pepper. Toss to combine, and serve immediately.

Sautéed Peas with Radishes and Scallions

Ingredients:

1 ½ Tablespoons of unsalted butter

3/4 pound snap peas, strings removed

8 scallions, diced

8 radishes cut into wedges

Salt and ground pepper

1 clove of garlic, finely minced

Directions: In a large skillet, heat butter over medium-high heat. Add snap peas and garlic , cook, tossing frequently, until just beginning to soften, 3 to 4 minutes. Add scallions and radishes; season with salt and pepper. Cook, tossing frequently, until scallions soften and snap peas are crisp-tender.

Rice with Peas and Cilantro

Ingredients:

1 cup fresh cilantro, chopped

2 Tablespoons extra-virgin olive oil

1 medium onion, finely chopped

1 garlic clove, minced

1/4 teaspoon chili powder

Coarse salt and freshly ground pepper

1 cup long-grain rice

1 1/2 cups water

1 pound fresh English peas, shelled (1 1/2 cups)

Directions: Heat oil in a pot over medium heat. Cook onion and garlic, stirring occasionally, until tender. Add chili powder, and season with salt and pepper; cook for 1 minute. Add rice, and stir to coat. Add the water; bring to a boil. Reduce heat to low, and gently simmer, covered, until water is absorbed, about 15 minutes. Remove from heat, and add peas (do not mix). Cover, and let stand for 10 minutes Season with salt and pepper. Stir in cilantro.

Glazed Snow Peas

Ingredients:

2 Tablespoons of butter

1 ½ cups of snow peas

1 bunch of scallions

A pinch of sugar

salt and pepper

¼ a cup of water

Directions: Melt 2 tablespoons butter in a large skillet over medium-high heat. Add snow peas, 1 bunch chopped scallions, a pinch of sugar and 1/4 cup water. Cover and simmer 2 minutes, then uncover and boil until the water evaporates, 2 more minutes. Season with salt.

Snow Pea and Radish Slaw

Ingredients:

1 red onion, thinly sliced

1 bunch of radishes, thinly sliced

4 teaspoons of rice vinegar

½ teaspoon of Dijon mustard

½ teaspoon of sugar

2 Tablespoons of olive oil

½ teaspoon of sesame oil

1 cup of thinly sliced snow peas

Directions: Thinly slice red onion and radishes. Soak in ice water, 5 minutes; drain and pat dry. Whisk 4 teaspoons rice vinegar and 1/2 teaspoon each dijon mustard and sugar in a bowl. Whisk in 2 tablespoons vegetable oil and 1/2 teaspoon sesame oil. Add thinly sliced snow peas, the onion and radishes. Season with salt. To speed things up you can also use your food processor to slice the radishes and onion.

Peppers

Whether you like them spicy hot or super sweet, peppers are a staple in a Midwestern vegetable farm. They are relatively easy to grow, easy to cook with and easy to preserve. There is a big misconception about how peppers grow; at least to the general public. Red peppers don't start off as red. And if you buy a green pepper plant and the fruit suddenly turns red or orange that doesn't mean it's bad (I've known of people to dig up their "green pepper" plant because the peppers were turning red!) Green peppers are simply unripe peppers. If left on the plant, green peppers will turn a variety of colors! Red, orange or purple peppers are sweeter than green peppers because they are ripe! Also, the most nutrients can be found in red peppers but all around, peppers are loaded with nutrition!

Organic peppers are strides above regular peppers you find at the grocery store. You probably already know that conventional peppers are doused in synthetic pesticides and their super thin skins allow the chemicals to seep into the pepper. But did you also know that conventional peppers are covered in a petroleum-based wax to make them shine? (Healthy vegetables don't need "makeup" to make them more appealing!). This wax is toxic and doesn't come off when you rinse them.

Storing Peppers: Unwashed sweet peppers stored in the vegetable compartment of the refrigerator will keep for approximately 7-10 days. . Because bell peppers need to still be well hydrated and are very sensitive to moisture loss, I recommend that you include a damp cloth or paper towel in the vegetable compartment to help the peppers retain their moisture. Do not cut out the bell pepper stem prior to storage

Preserving Peppers: Freezing peppers is by far the easiest, but I've also dried them in a food dehydrator or strung cayenne peppers on a string to air dry. You don't need to blanch peppers before freezing, just cut into strips or dice and store in a freezer bag. Frozen peppers are excellent to add to chili! If you drying peppers, you'll want to reconstitute them and are best used in, again, chili or soups. You can dry hot peppers and grind them for your own cayenne powder, red pepper flakes, etc. Finally, roasting peppers is an excellent way to preserve a bunch and retain a ton of flavor. Here's CSA member Jennifer Swartout's version:

Jennifer's Roasted Peppers

Set oven on "broil" setting. Place peppers (hot or mild) on cookie sheet (you may line the sheet with aluminum foil; can help with clean up). You can crowd them on the sheet; as long as they're not overlapping they're in good shape.

Broil the peppers until they really start getting blackened in spots. Then flip them to the other side. (You really need to get most of the pepper roasted/blackened for this to work).

Once the peppers are roasted on most sides, use tongs to move them to a very large bowl. Set a dinner-sized plate on top of the bowl – you're doing this to trap the heat and steam inside. Steaming the peppers really helps to get the skins off.

After about 10 minutes, remove the plate and let the peppers cool.

Once you're able to handle the peppers, you may slip the skins off. Be careful! Don't burn your hands. Be patient.

I usually do this for large quantities, and then freeze them in sandwich-sized bags for the off-season!

Favorite easy things to do with roasted peppers: Add a bunch to homemade spaghetti sauce; puree (add a wee bit of salt) and serve with pita wedges and hummus.

Zesty Mexican Soup

Ingredients:

1 medium onion, minced

4 medium cloves garlic, chopped

2 Tablespoons of red chili powder

3 cups + 1 Tablespoon of chicken or vegetable broth

1 small to medium green bell pepper, diced into 1/4-inch pieces

1 small zucchini, diced into 1/4-inch pieces

1 cup finely chopped collard greens

1 cup of diced tomatoes

2 cups black beans, rinsed

1 cup yellow corn (fresh or frozen)

1 4 oz can diced green chili

1 teaspoon of dried oregano

1 teaspoon of ground cumin

1/4 cup chopped pumpkin seeds

1/2 cup chopped fresh cilantro

salt and pepper to taste

Directions: Heat 1 Tablespoon of broth in a medium soup pot. Sauté onion, garlic, and green peppers in broth over medium heat for about 5 minutes, stirring often.
Add red chili powder and mix in well. Add broth and tomatoes. Cook for another 5 minutes and add beans, corn, green chili, oregano, and cumin.

Bring to a boil on high heat. Once it begins to boil, reduce heat to medium-low and simmer uncovered for 10 minutes longer. Add zucchini and collard greens and cook for 5 more minutes. Add chopped cilantro, pumpkin seeds, salt, and pepper.

Red Bell Pepper Relish

This is SUPER easy and great spread on sandwiches or crackers, on a bagel with cream cheese, or smeared over brie.

Ingredients:

1 red bell pepper (or any other type of bell pepper), chopped in small pieces

1/2 onion, chopped in small pieces

2/3 cup of sugar

1/2 cup of white vinegar

1/2 teaspoon of red pepper flakes

Directions: Add everything to a small sauce pan and stir all the ingredients until well incorporated. Cook the relish on medium heat for 5 minutes and turn down the heat to medium-low for an additional 20 minutes, stirring occasionally until most of the liquid has reduced. Remove from heat and allow to cool before serving.

Sausage with Peppers and Onions

This is one of my go-to meals to feed farm hands. It's super easy and makes the house smell amazing. As I stand at the stove cooking my peppers and onions I like to think it brings this farm girl just a little closer to her Chicago roots. The recipe is really loose in terms of quantity of ingredients. Use as much or little of anything as you like.
Ingredients:
One package of Italian Sausage links
5 bell peppers, sliced
5 onions, sliced
3 cloves of garlic, finely minced.
1 teaspoon of fresh thyme, leaves removed and chopped
1 Tablespoon of olive oil
4 Tablespoons of butter

Directions: In a large pan over medium heat added olive oil and melt butter until it starts to foam. Then add sliced onions, garlic and peppers and cook until the house smells amazing. Actually, cook until they turn tender and the onions start to brown. Set aside.

Meanwhile grill your sausages or pan fry them until almost done. Add the sausages to your peppers and onions and combine. Add thyme. Cook on low for 10 minutes while the flavors meld together. I've been known to pour some beer over the sausages. You can keep these in a covered pan on low in the oven or in a crock pot until ready to serve.

Stuffed Peppers
One of my favorites from my mom, Susan Johnson.
Ingredients:
4 bell peppers
1 pound of hamburger browned and drained (you can also use ground pork or turkey too)
1 jar of tomato sauce
1 onion, diced
1 cup of minute rice (uncooked)
1 1/2 cups of shredded cheese (we use cheddar or mozzarella, the choice is yours)

Directions: Preheat oven to 350 F. Hollow peppers and remove a bit of the rounded bottoms so the stand up. Par boil for 2-3 minutes to soften. Place standing up in a shallow baking pan. Combine hamburger, sauce and rice and stuff in peppers, cover with foil.

Cook at 350 degrees for 20 minutes, remove foil, sprinkle with cheese and return to oven for 3-5 minutes more

Potatoes

Potatoes are more than just a starchy vegetable. They are a reminder to us as to why monocultures (a farming environment that grows one to two different types of crops consistently and lacks biodiversity) are so harmful. You see monocultures everywhere around you when you live in the Midwest. Corn. Soybeans. Corn. Soybeans. Usually all the same varieties. In Ireland it was the same cloned potato variety planted everywhere. They relied heavily on the potato and when blight struck the potato crops there were no more potatoes. People were starving. Promoting monocultures is stripping our food security. Most of the corn and soybeans grown in the Midwest aren't even edible. It's grown for animal feed, ethanol and as a food by-product (corn syrup, soybean oil). Small, organic vegetable farmers do the opposite. They plant lots of different crops and with each type of crop there are usually multiple varieties. If the potatoes get flooded, we've always got winter squash and onion. If the salad mix seeds won't germinate, we've got spinach or romaine head lettuce. Biodiversity is a way to ensure nature's balance.

Storing potatoes: Keep in a cool, dark place. Potatoes will last quite a long time if you store them correctly.

Preserving potatoes: Canning potatoes? Nah. Drying potatoes? It's possible, but takes a while. Freezing them? Yep. It's totally possible. But you have to do it right or else you end up with mush. First, you don't want to freeze raw potatoes. You have to blanch or lightly bake them first. It's also useful to actually cut the potatoes into the shape you plan on using later. Example: shredded for hashbrowns, wedged for fries, etc. Here's how:

To freeze potatoes for hash browns, shred potatoes; hold in a bowl of cold water until all potatoes are shredded. Drain and blanch in boiling water about 3 minutes. Drain, rinse in cold water, drain again and pat dry. Pack into freezer bags. For fries, cut potatoes and hold in cold water until all potatoes are cut. Blanch in boiling water for 2 minutes; plunge into cold water; drain and dry well with paper towels. Bake at 375° until very light brown. Cool and pack into freezer containers or bags. Later, bake in an oven preheated to 375° until crisp and golden brown.

Potato with/Leek Vinaigrette

Ingredients:

4 leeks

4 medium potatoes

1 red bell pepper

Vinaigrette:

1/2 cup olive oil

1/4 cup vinegar

1 garlic clove, minced

1 1/2 teaspoons chopped fresh dill

salt and pepper to taste

Directions: Wash the leeks well. Slice the bulb and the tender green parts into 1/2 inch pieces. Drop the sliced leeks into boiling water, cook them for about 5 minutes, drain, and set aside to cool.

Cut the potatoes into 1 1/2 inch chunks. Drop them into boiling, salted water and cook until tender, but firm, about 10 minutes. Drain and set aside. Slice the red pepper into 1 inch strips.

Whisk together the vinaigrette ingredients. Then combine the leeks, potatoes, and peppers in a serving bowl. Pour on the vinaigrette and chill well before serving.

German Potato Salad

It's only fitting that I include this recipe considering my husband's name is Johann.

Ingredients:

2 pounds Yukon Gold or yellow potatoes, unpeeled

1/2 pound bacon

1 large white onion, chopped

2 Tablespoons safflower or canola oil

3 Tablespoons whole-grain mustard

6 Tablespoons apple cider vinegar, or to taste

1 bunch green onions, chopped

1/2 teaspoon salt

1/2 teaspoon ground black pepper

2 Tablespoons fresh parsley, chopped

Directions: Boil potatoes in a large pot until tender, 15 to 20 minutes. Don't let them get too soft—a fork should go in but potatoes should not fall apart. Drain and cool slightly, then peel if desired and slice. Meanwhile, cook bacon in a large skillet over medium heat until crisp; transfer to a paper towel-lined plate to let drain. When cool enough to handle, crumble into small pieces. Drain off all but 1 tablespoon fat from the skillet, then return to medium heat. Add white onion and cook until lightly browned, 7 to 8 minutes. In a large bowl, gently toss together warm bacon, potatoes and white onion with oil, mustard, vinegar, green onions, salt and pepper. Garnish with parsley and serve warm or at room temperature.

Potato Basil Mash

Ingredients:

2 cups fresh basil leaves, lightly packed

2 pounds potatoes

1 cup half-and-half

¾ cup grated Parmesan cheese, plus extra for serving

2 teaspoons salt

1 teaspoon ground black pepper

Directions: Bring a large pot of salted water to boil and fill a bowl with ice water. Add the basil leaves to the boiling water and blanch for 15 seconds. Remove the basil with a slotted spoon and immediately plunge the leaves into the ice water to stop the cooking process. Drain and set aside. Peel the potatoes and cut them in quarters. Add the potatoes to the same pot of boiling water and return to a boil. Cook the potatoes for 20 to 25 minutes, until very tender. Drain well.

In a small saucepan over medium heat, heat the half-and-half and Parmesan cheese until the cream simmers. Place the basil in a food processor fitted with the steel blade and purée. Add the hot cream mixture and process until smooth. Mash the hot potatoes in the pot, either with a hand-help mixer or with a potato masher, until they are broken up. Slowly add the hot basil cream, the salt, and pepper and mix until smooth. Pour into a serving bowl, sprinkle with extra Parmesan cheese, season to taste, and serve hot.

Potato Fennel Casserole

For some reason potatoes and fennel are like peas and carrots. They just go really well together!

Ingredients:

2 small fennel bulbs

1 onion, thinly sliced

1 teaspoon of fresh thyme, chopped

2 Tablespoons olive oil

1 Tablespoon unsalted butter

2 pounds of potatoes (about 4 large potatoes)

2 cups plus 2 tablespoons heavy cream

2 1/2 cups grated cheddar cheese

1 teaspoon salt

1/2 teaspoon ground black pepper

Directions: Preheat the oven to 350 degrees and butter the inside of a baking dish (I use 11X13) Remove the stalks from the fennel and cut the bulbs in half lengthwise. Remove the cores and thinly slice the bulbs. Sauté the fennel, thyme and onions in the olive oil and butter on medium-low heat for 15 minutes, until tender. Peel the potatoes, then thinly slice them by hand or with a mandoline.

Mix the sliced potatoes in a large bowl with 2 cups of cream, 2 cups of cheese salt, and pepper. Add the sautéed fennel and onion and mix well. Pour the potatoes into the baking dish. Combine the remaining 2 tablespoons of cream and 1/2 cup of cheese and sprinkle on the top. Bake for 1 1/2 hours, until the potatoes are very tender and the top is browned and bubbly. Allow to set for 10 minutes and serve.

Potato Leek Soup

Ingredients:

4 medium leeks, dark green tops removed

3 Tablespoons unsalted butter

3 small, Yukon gold potatoes, peeled and diced small

1 quart vegetable broth

1 cup heavy cream

1 cup buttermilk

1/2 teaspoon pepper

1 Tablespoon snipped chives

1 teaspoon of salt

Directions: Wash the leeks well and chop into small pieces. In a saucepan or dutch oven over medium heat, melt the butter. Add the leeks and a heavy pinch of salt and sauté for 5 minutes. Decrease the heat to medium-low and cook until the leeks are tender, approximately 25 minutes, stirring occasionally.

Add the potatoes and broth, increase the heat to medium-high, and bring to a boil. Reduce the heat to low, cover, and gently simmer until the potatoes are soft, approximately 45 minutes.

Turn off the heat and puree the mixture with an immersion blender, hand mixer or in batches in your regular blender until smooth. Stir in the heavy cream, buttermilk, and pepper. Taste and adjust seasoning if desired. Sprinkle with chives and serve warm.

Vegan Potato Leek Soup

Ingredients:

6 medium potatoes, diced

2 large leeks, dark green tops removed

1/2 yellow onion

2 cloves garlic

2 Tablespoons olive oil

3 Tablespoons white wine

1/2 teaspoon of thyme

1/2 teaspoon of rosemary

4 cups vegetable broth

1 teaspoon of salt & black pepper to taste

1 cup plain soy or almond milk

Directions: Rinse the leeks and thinly slice. Heat the oil in your large stockpot and sauté the leeks and onions for a 10 minutes until tender. Add the wine and garlic. Sauté for another 5 minutes more.

Add diced potatoes, water, broth, salt, pepper and herbs. Simmer until the potatoes are very soft, about 20 minutes. Use your immersion blender or a countertop blender to puree while slowing adding the soy or almond milk. Adjust salt and pepper to taste.

Pumpkin

Pumpkins aren't just for decoration! Pumpkin is great for many, many reasons. First... it lasts for months! Second, it's interchangeable with any winter squash recipe so it's easy to use. Third, it's packed with nutrients. It's loaded with Vitamin A, Carotenoids, Antioxidants, and has been known to regulate blood sugar!

I once attended a local organic farmer's harvest potluck

and tried this Japanese pumpkin stew dish that was served over jasmine rice. I loved it so much I came back for seconds and thirds. Not a month goes by that I don't think about that stew and curse myself for not asking around for who made it so I could get the recipe.

Storing Pumpkins: Easy. Cool. Dark. Done. They will last months and months.

Preserving Pumpkins: Because they last so long, rarely is there a need to preserve them, but if you find yourself elbow deep in pumpkins here's how to put them up for later:

Preheat your oven to 400F. Cut the squash in half and scoop out the seeds. Place the squash halves cut side down in a baking dish and pour in 1/2-inch of water.

Bake until the flesh of the squash is cooked (the peel will be starting to get brown spots). About 40-60 minutes. Let the squash cool and then scoop out the cooked flesh with a spoon.

At this point you can freeze the cooked squash as is or puree it either in the food processor or by mashing thoroughly with a potato masher. Do not add liquid when you puree the pulp. Pack the cooked squash into freezer bags and place in the freezer.

Maple Roasted Pumpkin

Ingredients

1 small pumpkin (2-3 pounds)

Maple syrup

Salt and pepper

Directions: Preheat oven to 400F. Cut pumpkin in half; scoop out seeds. Cut halves into 2 or 3 wedges depending on size of pumpkin.

Place skin side down on roasting pan. Cover with foil; bake

15 minutes or until pumpkins are fork tender.
Drizzle with maple syrup and sprinkle with salt and
pepper. Bake, uncovered, 15 minutes or until browned.

Pumpkin Chowder

Ingredients:
3 Tablespoons of olive oil
2 Leek chopped with green tops removed, trimmed of
tough green tops and chopped
3 large garlic cloves, minced
2 medium bell peppers, chopped
2 1/4 pounds pumpkin, peeled, seeded, and cut into 1/2- by
1-inch-thick pieces
1 teaspoon marjoram
1/4 teaspoon crushed red pepper
2 bay leaves
1/4 teaspoon salt
1/4 teaspoon ground black pepper
1 1/4 cup frozen corn
6 cups of vegetable broth or chicken broth

Directions: Heat olive oil in a large pot or Dutch oven over
medium heat. Add leeks and cook until very soft, about 5
minutes. Add garlic and cook for about 2 minutes. Stir in
green peppers, reduce heat to medium-low, and cook until
peppers soften, about 8 more minutes. Add the remaining
ingredients and cook until pumpkin is tender, about 30
minutes.

Sweet and Sour Grilled Pumpkin

Ingredients:

1 – 1 1/2 pound pumpkin

2 Tablespoons olive oil

1 clove garlic, minced

salt

3 Tablespoons red or white wine vinegar

3 tablespoons sugar

chopped fresh mint or parsley

Directions: Cut Pumpkin in half and scrape out the seeds. Peel each half and cut into 1/4-1/2 inch slices. In a large bowl, whisk together olive oil, minced garlic, and a good pinch of salt. Add pumpkin slices and toss well to coat. Grill pumpkin slices over medium to medium-heat for a few minutes on each side or until just tender. Watch closely and don't let them burn. Remove grilled pumpkin to a serving platter.

In a small saucepan, mix vinegar, sugar, and any garlic oil left in the bowl you tossed the pumpkin in. Cook until sugar is dissolved and mixture thickens just slightly. Drizzle sweet and sour sauce over the pumpkin on the serving platter. Garnish with fresh chopped mint or parsley. Serve warm or at room temperature.

Spicy Roasted Pumpkin Seeds

One of my fondest memories of autumn as a child are roasting pumpkin seeds after we carved our jack-o-lanterns.

Ingredients:

2 cups of Pumpkin Seeds

Olive Oil

1 Tablespoon of red pepper flakes,

1/2 teaspoon of cayenne pepper,

1 clove garlic, finely chopped,

1/4 teaspoon of salt.

Directions: Preheat oven to 350°F. Scoop out the inside of your squash, and separate seeds from pulp. Don't worry if there's a little pulp left on the seeds when you roast them – it only adds flavor. Just remove the biggest pieces so that the seeds are easy to toss. In a bowl, toss the seeds with melted butter or oil, coating thoroughly.

Add Seasonings. Spread seeds in one even layer across a greased baking sheet (or you can use a cookie sheet covered in aluminum foil). Bake until the seeds are golden brown, about 20 minutes. Stir the seeds every so often while they're baking, so that they toast evenly.

R

Radishes

One day at the farmers market a French woman was asking what the name was of particular radish that was long with a pinkish hue and a white tip. We told her it was called a French Breakfast radish. She scoffed and said "We don't eat those for breakfast!"

Truthfully, there are many different varieties of radishes with differences in color, shape and taste. They are all a delight to eat, but radishes get a bad reputation as being bitter, spicy or tough. Not the case if you're eating freshly dug, spring or fall radishes. As the temperature warms up radishes get pithy and have a spicy kick that most folks don't enjoy. People also think radishes are only for salads but again, this is a misconception. There are many uses for radishes that will liven up your weekly menu!

Storing radishes: If the leafy radish tops are attached, remove them before storing. Radishes don't keep as well if their tops are left on. Then store unwashed radishes in a bag in the refrigerator crisper drawer. Wash radishes and trim their roots just before using.

Preserving radishes: I've found the best way to preserve radishes is to pickle them.

Here's an easy way:

Quick Pickled Radishes
Ingredients:
1 1/2 cups radishes
10 fl oz white vinegar
10 peppercorns
2 teaspoons salt
2 teaspoons sugar (optional, or use honey, stevia, etc.)
1 small onion
1 bay leaf

Directions: Slice up radishes and onion. Bring vinegar, peppercorns, sugar and salt to a boil. Place radishes, onion and bay leaf into a clean mason jar. Pour vinegar mixture over radishes. Refrigerate overnight. Makes 1 pint.

Roasted Potato and Radish Salad

Ingredients:

1 large Yukon gold potato, cut into bite sized pieces

8-10 radishes, can be a variety of sizes and types, green tops removed and ends trimmed.

Extra virgin olive oil

Salt

Freshly ground black pepper

1/2 teaspoon ground mustard

1/2 teaspoon cumin

2 Tablespoons greek yogurt

2 Tablespoons thinly sliced green onions

2 Tablespoons lemon juice mixed with ½ t salt and ½ t sugar in a small bowl, until salt and sugar are dissolved

Directions: Preheat oven to 400 degrees. In a medium sized bowl, combine potato pieces with a tablespoon of olive oil, a sprinkling of salt, and a few grinds of black pepper, tossing evenly to coat. Roast potatoes in a single layer on a baking sheet for 10 minutes.

While the potatoes are roasting, halve and slice radishes into wedges. Using the same bowl that you tossed the potatoes in, combine radishes with another tablespoon of olive oil, salt and black pepper; mix well to evenly coat. Once the potatoes have roasted for 10 minutes, gently slide the potatoes to one side of pan, adding radishes in a single layer to the other side. Continue to roast for another 10-12 minutes or until potatoes and radishes are tender.

Remove pan from oven and allow vegetables to cool. Transfer roasted radishes and potatoes to a bowl. Add greek yogurt, mustard, cumin and green onions, folding with a spatula to combine. Add lemon juice mixture by the teaspoonful until you reach desired taste. I added one and a half teaspoons of lemon juice-salt-sugar mixture. Fold to combine. Cover mixture with plastic wrap and refrigerate for at least an hour.

Radish Greens Soup

tasty!

Ingredients:

4 Tablespoons unsalted butter
1 large yellow onion, cut into 1/4-inch dice
2 bunches radish greens (about 2 cups), cleaned
6 medium baking potatoes, peeled and cut into 1/2-inch dice
4 1/2 cups Chicken Stock
1 cup heavy cream (I've used half and half too and it turned out lovely)
salt and pepper
5 radishes, finely grated or zested

Directions: In a medium stockpot, melt butter over medium heat. Stir in onions, and saute until transparent, about 4 minutes. Add radish greens, and cook until wilted, about 4 minutes. Add potatoes and chicken stock, and cook, stirring occasionally, until potatoes are tender, about 35 minutes.
Working in batches, pass the mixture through a food mill into a medium bowl. Stir in cream, and season with salt and pepper. Strain the pureed mixture through a fine-mesh sieve into the original pot. Bring soup just to a simmer over medium heat. Serve with zested radishes for garnish.

Roasted Radishes

Ingredients:

Radishes, washed with the tops removed
Extra-virgin olive oil
salt and pepper
Fresh lemon juice

Directions: Preheat oven to 450F. Toss radishes with oil. Season with salt and pepper. Roast on a baking sheet, stirring once, until slightly tender and browned, about 15 minutes. Sprinkle with salt. Drizzle with lemon juice.

Mama Jeffers Radish Sandwich
Ingredients:
Radishes
White bread
Butter
Salt

Directions: Slice your garden fresh radishes and place on buttered white bread, sprinkle with a little salt and enjoy.

Rutabaga

Fun to say and tasty to eat! The rutabaga is sometimes confused with a turnip and rightly so. Rutabagas originated as a cross between the turnip and the cabbage. Rutabagas are one of those hearty winter crops that will store for a long time. Rutabagas also contain lots of vitamin C! So why do so many people refuse to give rutabaga's a try? Sure the name isn't very appealing. The word Rutabaga reminds me of carburetor and car parts aren't generally appetizing. (Luckily they are also known as "Swedes" which does sound more appetizing!) Or maybe it's because back in the old day rutabagas were considered a "famine food" because they were easy to grow and stored for long periods of time. I urge you to keep an open mind about the mighty rutabaga, you won't be disappointed.

Storing Rutabagas: When you get your rutabagas home remove the green tops and store in a bag in your crisper drawer

Preserving Rutabagas: Since properly stored rutabagas can last as long as 4 months, preserving them is really unnecessary. Plus, canning rutabagas usually creates a strange, "strong" taste. Freezing them usually just gives you mushy rutabagas and dehydrating them may also change their texture quite a bit.

Rutabaga Gratin

Ingredients:

6 Tablespoons of butter

¼ of a yellow onion, finely diced

4 cups peeled and grated rutabaga

3 eggs

3 oz cream cheese

2 cups of milk

3/4 teaspoon salt

Pepper to taste

3/4 cups of bread crumbs

Directions: Melt 3 Tablespoons of butter in a large sauté pan and cook onion until lightly colored; add grated rutabaga. Stir to coat with butter and cook until wilted, 8-10 minutes. Meanwhile in a separate bowl, beat eggs, add cream cheese, and beat together thoroughly. Heat milk in a saucepan to a light simmer and gradually add to egg mixture. Then stir in the rutabaga mixture, salt, and pepper. Pour into a buttered 8x8 inch ovenproof dish. Melt remaining 3 Tablespoons of butter in a pan, sauté bread crumbs for 30 to-60 seconds, and top the rutabaga mixture with them. Bake for 30 minutes in a preheated 350 degree oven.

Raw Rutabaga Salad

Ingredients:

1 whole rutabaga, peeled

1 orange

1/4 cup raisins

Directions: Grate the rutabaga on a mandolin or large side of a grater, put the strips to a bowl. Peel the orange and cut it into 2/3 inch-ish wide pieces and mix the juicy pieces with rutabaga. Add some raisins.

Farmhouse Chowder

Adapted from Martha Stewart

Ingredients:

1 whole chicken (3 1/2 to 4 pounds)

6 cups of water

4 cups of chicken stock

2 carrots, diced

½ a medium yellow onion, diced

1 ounce (2 tablespoons) unsalted butter

2 Tablespoons flour

1 small turnip, cut into 1/2-inch dice

1 rutabaga, cut into 1/2-inch dice

salt

1/2 cup heavy cream

Directions: Place chicken, breast side down, in a large pot. Add water and stock. Bring to a boil, partially covered. Reduce heat, and simmer gently for 1 hour. Remove chicken, and let cool. Strain broth through a fine sieve and return broth to the pot and set aside.. Shred chicken into bite-size pieces, discarding bones and skin.

Melt butter in a large pot over medium heat. Add chopped onion and diced carrot, and cook until onion is translucent, about 5 minutes. Stir in flour, and cook, stirring, for 1 minute. Whisk chicken broth, and bring to a boil. Add turnip and rutabaga , and 2 1/2 teaspoons salt. Reduce heat, and simmer until root vegetables are tender, 6 to 8 minutes.

Stir in reserved chicken and the cream, and heat until warmed through, about 1 minute. Season with salt.

Smoky Mashed Rutabaga

Ingredients:

3 1/2 to 4 pounds rutabagas (two small or one large)
2 Tablespoons unsalted butter
4 garlic cloves, peeled and roughly chopped
1 1/2 teaspoons salt
1 cup whole milk
4 ounces cream cheese, cut into small chunks
2 Tablespoons olive oil
1 ½ teaspoons of ground nutmeg
2 teaspoons smoked paprika
ground black pepper

Directions: Cut off the green tops and peel the rutabagas. Cut the peeled rutabaga into small slices about 1 inch thick. Melt the butter in a large pot, over medium heat. When the butter has melted, stir in the chopped rutabaga and the garlic. Stir to coat the vegetables in butter, then sprinkle them with the salt. Pour in the milk and bring to a simmer, then turn the heat to low and cover the pot. Cook for 35 minutes, or until the rutabaga is very tender and can be easily pierced with a fork. Turn off the heat and remove the lid. Let the vegetables cool for about 5 minutes.

Use a hand mixer or immersion blender to whip the mixture. Drop the cream cheese into the rutabaga and continue to mix. The rutabaga will crumble then slowly turn into a mashed potato consistency. Add the olive oil, nutmeg and smoked paprika and mix thoroughly. Taste and add more salt and some black pepper, if necessary. Serve immediately.

S

Spinach

Growing up as a kid I never had fresh spinach. Actually, I'm pretty sure I never had fresh spinach until I started farming with Hans in my early 30's. I had eaten canned spinach and frozen spinach and both types have left no memorable impressions. Spinach was never something I'd buy in the grocery store. The word "spinach" never left my lips. I never, ever thought about spinach. Now I eat spinach on a weekly basis. I love to throw some into my spaghetti sauce about 5 minutes before I'm ready to serve it. It goes in just about any salad I make. I layer it into my lasagna, throw it in my soups, make spinach quiche or just sauté it with garlic as a side dish. The possibilities are endless. I see no reason to ever eat frozen or canned spinach again.

Storing spinach: Don't wash your spinach before you store it. Just place in a bag and store in your refrigerator. Should last up to a week.

Preserving spinach: Hands down, best way of preserving spinach is to freeze it. Rinse the spinach well. Bring enough water to cover your spinach to a boil. When the water is boiling throw in the spinach. Blanch for 2 minutes. As soon as time is up remove spinach to a bowl ice water. Drain the spinach. Package the spinach in freezer bags. Flatten the spinach out in the baggie and squeeze out as much air as possible. Label and freeze flat.

Easy Spinach Dip

Ingredients:

1 quart size bag of frozen spinach, thawed and drained (or use 2 cups of fresh spinach and lightly sauté in olive oil until wilted).

1 cup sour cream

1/2 cup mayonnaise

1 packet onion soup mix

pepper to taste

Directions: Mix together all ingredients thoroughly. Chill for at least an hour before serving to allow flavors to mingle. That's it!

Katie's Spinach Quiche

This freezes well and is great any time of the day! You can make your own crust or use a frozen, pre-made crust like I do:

Ingredients:

1 3-ounce package cream cheese, room temperature

1/3 cup half and half

3 eggs (from PrairiErth Farm... I hope! :)

1 cup of roughly chopped spinach

1/2 cup grated cheddar

1/4 cup grated Parmesan

4 to 6 green onions, sliced

1/4 teaspoon salt

1/4 teaspoon pepper

Directions: Preheat oven to 425°F. Beat cream cheese in medium bowl until smooth. Gradually beat in half and half and eggs. Mix in remaining ingredients. Pour mixture into prepared crust. Bake until crust is golden brown and filling is set, about 25 minutes. Cool 10 minutes before serving.

Spinach Lasagna Rolls

This is a way to control portions and is very freezer friendly. Ingredients:

9 lasagna noodles, cooked

1 cup of spinach, washed/stems removed & leaves roughly chopped

1 (15 ounce) container of ricotta cheese

1/2 cup grated Parmesan cheese

1 egg

1/2 teaspoon minced garlic

1/2 teaspoon dried Italian seasoning

salt and fresh pepper

1 jar of tomato sauce

1 cup of grated mozzarella

Directions: Preheat oven to 350°. Combine spinach, ricotta, Parmesan cheese, egg, garlic, Italian seasonings and salt and pepper in a medium bowl. Pour about 1 cup sauce on the bottom of a 9 x 13 baking dish. Place a cookie sheet or large platter on the counter and lay out lasagna noodles. Make sure noodles are dry by patting them with a towel.

Take 1/3 cup of ricotta mixture and spread evenly over a noodle. Roll carefully and place seam side down onto the baking dish. Repeat with remaining noodles. Ladle sauce over the noodles in the baking dish and top each one with mozzarella cheese. Cover baking dish tightly with aluminum foil and bake for 40 minutes, or until cheese melts. Makes 9 rolls.

Sautéed Garlic Spinach

Adapted From the Barefoot Contessa

Ingredients:

1 1/2 pounds baby spinach leaves

2 Tablespoons olive oil

2 Tablespoons chopped garlic (6 cloves)

2 teaspoons salt

3/4 teaspoon ground black pepper

1 Tablespoon unsalted butter

Lemon

Directions: Rinse the spinach well in cold water to make sure it's very clean. Spin it dry in a salad spinner. In a very large pot or Dutch oven, heat the olive oil and sauté the garlic over medium heat for about 1 minute, but not until it's browned. Add all the spinach, the salt, and pepper to the pot, toss it with the garlic and oil, cover the pot, and cook it for 2 minutes.

Uncover the pot, turn the heat on high, and cook the spinach for another minute, stirring with a wooden spoon, until all the spinach is wilted. Using a slotted spoon, lift the spinach to a serving bowl and top with the butter, a squeeze of lemon, and a sprinkling of salt. Serve hot.

Spanakopita (Greek Spinach Pie)

I swear, I am part Greek. I'm actually part Croatian which isn't that far from Greece, but at any rate I LOVE Greek food. So here's a dish straight from my Greek recipe archives. It takes a little work and a slow hand but is very worth it.

Ingredients:

1 pound (or more!) fresh spinach (feel free to substitute some of the spinach with chard, kale, turnip greens, or arugula)

5 oz feta cheese, crumbled

1/2 cup fresh dill (chopped and then measured)

3 green onions, chopped

2 eggs

salt/pepper to taste

1/4 to 1/3 cup olive oil

Phyllo dough, thawed overnight in the fridge (you can get this in the freezer section of most grocery stores)

Directions: Steam or blanch the spinach till it wilts. Run under cold water to stop cooking process. Then lightly squeeze the spinach and drain. Chop the cooked spinach into small pieces. Mix spinach, feta, dill, green onions, eggs, salt, and pepper in a large bowl.

Brush the bottom of an 8×8 pan with olive oil (9×13 also works). Brush the top of a sheet of phyllo with oil and place in pan. Fold phyllo over to fit in pan. Repeat until you have 6-8 layers of phyllo (more or less, depending on how thick you want the crust). Phyllo can be very fragile so just be gentle, take it slow and make sure it's completely thawed.

Spread the spinach mixture on top of the phyllo crust. Brush the top of another sheet of phyllo with oil and place on top of spinach. Repeat till you have 6-8 layers. Finish by brushing the top layer of phyllo with oil.

Cut your unbaked spanakopita into squares or triangles with a sharp knife. Bake in a preheated 350F oven until golden brown on top, about 30-50 minutes.

Summer Squash

There are two things a farmer must do when the summer squash starts to come on. Clip their finger nails and get out the cookbook. First the nails... it's a hard lesson to learn, but if you don't cut your nails really short you will pierce the skin of the squash each time you pick it up. It's inevitable. Their skin is very, very thin! So when it's time to go harvest I have to do a finger nail check!
But the cookbook chore is more fun. Sometimes coming up with what to do with all your summer squash can be overwhelming. We usually revert to just grilling it. I've got a good recipe so it always tastes great, but there are also some really yummy ways to utilize that bounty of summer squash!

Storing summer squash: Wrap tightly in a bag and store in the fridge immediately. Do not wash until you're ready to use it.
Preserving summer squash: You can always freeze your summer squash! (Running out of freezer space yet!?) I usually shred some for breads and soups and dice some for other dishes.
There is much debate about canning summer squash or zucchini. The USDA does not promote canning these types of vegetables due to outbreaks in botulism with canned squash. They won't even provide processing times. So can at your own risk.

Stuffed Summer Squash

Ingredients:

2 teaspoons salt, plus more to taste

2 1/2 pounds small to medium yellow crookneck squash (about 8 to 10 squash)

2 Tablespoons olive oil

1 cup finely diced onion

2 garlic cloves, minced

1 cup finely diced button mushrooms (or any mushrooms you'd like)

1 1/2 cups crumbled queso fresco (I've used feta too and it worked great!)

1/4 cup plus 1 teaspoon finely chopped parsley

ground black pepper

Directions: Heat the oven to 350 degrees. In a medium pot, bring water to a boil, then add 2 teaspoons salt and the squash. Reduce the heat and simmer the squash, covered, until they are just tender when pierced with a knife, about 8 to 10 minutes (timing will vary depending on the size of the squash). Drain the squash and chill in a bowl of ice water until cool to the touch.

Halve each squash lengthwise, and scoop out the flesh in the center with a spoon, making sure to leave enough flesh near the shell so the shells can be stuffed. Place the scooped flesh in a strainer and set aside to drain for at least 10 minutes to drain excess liquid.

While the squash is draining, heat a medium pan over medium-high heat. Add the oil, then the onion and garlic and sauté until the onion is softened and translucent, 3 to 4 minutes. Stir in the mushrooms and continue to cook until they are tender and lightly browned, another 5 to 6 minutes. Stir in the drained squash flesh (don't worry if it is still moist, it will not be completely dry) and stir well to combine, scraping any browned bits from the bottom of the pan. Remove from heat and set the squash filling aside to cool slightly.

In a medium bowl, combine the squash filling, queso fresco and 1/4 cup parsley. Stir well and season with a generous 1/4 teaspoon salt and several grinds of pepper.
Divide the filling into the squash shells. Place the shells in a large baking dish and bake until hot and lightly browned in spots, 25 to 35 minutes depending on the size of the squash. Sprinkle with the remaining 1 teaspoon of parsley and serve.

Squash and Onions with Brown Sugar
Ingredients:
2 medium yellow squash
1 medium onion
2 Tablespoons unsalted butter
1 teaspoon salt
1/2 teaspoon pepper
1 1/2 Tablespoons brown sugar

Directions: Slice the squash into 1/2-inch rounds, You should end up with roughly 2 cups of cut squash. Cut the onions into similar-sized slices.
Add the butter to a wide sauce pan that has a lid and heat over medium heat. When the butter has melted, add the onions and cook until soft, about 4-5 minutes. Add squash, salt, pepper, and brown sugar. Stir, then cover and cook for about 20 minutes, until squash is very soft.
Remove the cover and continue to cook for about 8 minutes, just to give the juices a chance to evaporate slightly. There will be some liquid in the pan, but it should be thicker than water, almost like a glaze. Season with more salt and pepper, if needed, and serve immediately.

Summer Squash Bread

You've heard of zucchini bread... but this bread is a savory treat!

Ingredients:

1/4 cup olive oil, plus more for coating the pan

2 cups all-purpose flour

1/4 cup finely ground yellow cornmeal

2 teaspoons baking powder

1 1/4 teaspoons dried oregano

3/4 teaspoon fine salt

1/2 teaspoon baking soda

1/2 teaspoon freshly ground black pepper

2 large eggs

3/4 cup buttermilk

2 cups grated summer squash, such as round zucchini, pattypan, or crookneck (from about 1 pound squash)

2/3 cup finely crumbled feta cheese

Directions: Heat the oven to 350°F and arrange a rack in the middle. Generously coat a 9-by-5-inch loaf pan with olive oil; set aside.

Place flour, cornmeal, baking powder, oregano, salt, baking soda, and pepper in a large bowl and whisk until combined.

Place eggs, buttermilk, and 1/4 cup olive oil in a separate large bowl and whisk until smooth. Using a rubber spatula, fold in squash and feta until evenly combined. Pour squash mixture into flour mixture and stir until flour is just incorporated, being careful not to overmix (a few streaks of flour are OK).

Scrape the batter into the prepared loaf pan, pushing it into the corners and smoothing the top. Bake until the bread is golden brown all over and a toothpick inserted into it comes out clean (test several spots, because you may hit a pocket of cheese), about 60 to 65 minutes. Place the pan on a wire rack to cool for 15 minutes, then turn the bread out onto the rack and cool for at least 15 minutes more before serving.

Potato, Squash, and Goat Cheese Gratin

CSA member Sarah Hull
Ingredients:
2 medium yellow squash
4 small to medium red potatoes
3 Tablespoons olive oil
4 ounces goat cheese
salt and pepper
1/4 cup whole milk
1/3 cup freshly grated parmesan cheese
1 tablespoon thinly sliced basil, optional

Directions: Preheat oven to 400°F. Use a mandoline or chef's knife to slice the squash and potatoes into very, very thin slices, 1/8-inch or less. Toss the sliced vegetables with the olive oil in a large bowl.

Pour a small drizzle of olive oil in a casserole dish (around 8 or 9 inches square) and spread it around the bottom and sides. Place 1/3 of the squash and potato slices in the bottom of the dish—no need to layer them squash-potato-squash-etc.—then season with salt and pepper. Top with half of the goat cheese, scattered evenly in large chunks. Repeat with another 1/3 of the vegetables, seasoning again with salt and pepper and topping with the other 1/2 of the goat cheese. Finish by layering on the final 1/3 of the vegetables and seasoning with salt and pepper.

Pour the milk over the entire dish. Top with the parmesan cheese. Bake, covered, for 30 minutes, then uncover and bake 15 more minutes, until the top browns. Scatter on the fresh basil, if using.

Summer Squash and Corn Soup

I know the words "summer" and "soup" can make you cringe however if you do make this soup in the summer and freeze it for the cold winter months you will thank me. It's sunshine on a cloudy, frigid winter day. It will trick your tongue into thinking it's 80 degrees outside. It will make you smile. I promise! Just leave off the feta if you do freeze it.

Ingredients:

1 Tablespoon extra-virgin olive oil

1 medium onion, chopped

2 medium summer squash, (about 1 pound), diced

3 teaspoons chopped fresh herbs, such as thyme or oregano, divided

2 cups of chicken broth, or vegetable broth

1/4 teaspoon salt

1 cup fresh corn kernels

1 teaspoon lemon juice

1/4 cup crumbled feta cheese

Directions: Heat oil in a large saucepan or dutch oven over medium heat. Add diced onion and cook, stirring, 1 minute. Add squash and 1 teaspoon herbs and cook, stirring occasionally, until the squash starts to soften, 3 to 5 minutes.

Add broth and salt; bring to a boil. Reduce heat to a simmer and cook until the squash is soft and mostly translucent, about 5 minutes more. Transfer to a blender and puree until smooth or use an immersion blender. Return the soup to the pan and stir in corn. Bring to a simmer over medium heat and cook, stirring occasionally, until the corn is tender, 3 to 5 minutes more. Remove from the heat; stir in lemon juice. Serve garnished with the remaining 2 teaspoons herbs and feta. Makes about 4 cups.

Sweet Potato

Did you know that not all sweet potatoes are orange on the inside? They can be white or even purple! Although the orange ones are an excellent source of beta-carotene, the purple ones have properties that produce excellent anti-inflammatory benefits! The other great thing about sweet potatoes is their ability to regulate blood sugar. Yep, that's right. Usually, people think of starchy potatoes being nothing but carbs and therefore something diabetics should stay away from, but sweet potatoes can actually assist in regulating blood sugar!

Storing sweet potatoes: Sweet potatoes need to be kept in a cool, dry and dark place. The best thing you can do is to place them in a paper bag with some holes punched into it. Store the bag in a cupboard far away from anything producing heat like a dishwasher, oven or heating vent.
Preserving sweet potatoes: If you store them correctly, sweet potatoes will last for months. However, you can also can sweet potatoes as long as you have a pressure canner.

Spicy Sweet Potato Fries
Ingredients:
3 large sweet potatoes
2 Tablespoons of olive oil
1 Tablespoon of seasoning salt

Directions: Cut each sweet potato into slices about 1/4" thick. Toss the sweet potato slices with the oil and seasoning salt Spread out on baking sheets in a single layer.

Bake at 450 degrees for about 20-25 minutes, turning with a spatula as needed.

Sweet Potato Spoon Bread

A sweet and easy custard-like dish!

Ingredients:

3 large sweet potatoes

1/4 cup yellow cornmeal

2 cup milk

4 Tablespoons unsalted butter

1/4 cup light-brown sugar

1/4 teaspoon ground nutmeg

1/4 teaspoon ground cloves

1 1/2 teaspoon ground cinnamon

1 teaspoon salt

1/2 cup all-purpose flour

1/4 cup honey

4 large eggs

1 cup heavy cream

Directions: Heat oven to 400 degrees F. Bake sweet potatoes until soft when pierced with a knife, 40 to 45 minutes. Let cool. Peel, and discard skins.

Reduce heat to 350 degrees F. In a medium saucepan over medium heat combine cornmeal, milk, butter, brown sugar, spices, salt, and 1 cup water. Cook, stirring, until slightly thickened, about 10 minutes. Let cool.

Butter a 2-quart baking dish. Working in batches if necessary, place cornmeal mixture, sweet potatoes, flour, honey, eggs, and cream in a food processor. Process until smooth; pour into dish. Bake until golden brown, about 45 minutes. Serve.

Vegan Sweet Potato Biscuits with a Maple Glaze

Ingredients:

3 cups flour, whole wheat

1 cup warm water or soy milk

1 Tablespoon of baking powder

1 teaspoon of salt

1 medium sweet potato

2 Tablespoons of canola oil or vegan butter

2 Tablespoons of maple syrup

1 teaspoon of garlic powder

1 teaspoon of black pepper

a few dashes of cinnamon

Glaze:

3 Tablespoons of maple syrup

Directions: Combine dry ingredients in large bowl. Mix well.

Bake sweet potato, peel and mash in a separate bowl with the oil or vegan butter. Set aside. Add water (or soy milk) to the dry ingredients. Then spoon in the wet mashed sweet potato mixture. Fold by hand until a nice ball of dough is formed. Add more flour if dough is too sticky. Knead by hand on floured surface. Press out dough with fingers after kneading.

Use a biscuit cutter or a simple juice glass to cut out biscuits, transfer to parchment paper or greased cookie sheet. Warm the maple glaze in the microwave. Brush a light glaze onto each biscuit. Bake at 400 degrees for 20 minutes.

Southwest Sweet Potato Chowder

Cooked in a crockpot, this is a very easy recipe!

Ingredients:

3 large sweet potatoes, peeled and cut into 1 inch chunks

1 medium yellow onion, chopped

3 cloves garlic, diced

2 chipotle peppers, diced (this added the southwest heat, but it is optional)

2 teaspoons smoked paprika

1 teaspoon cumin

6 cups vegetable broth

1 Tablespoon apple cider vinegar

2 Tablespoons soy sauce

1 tablespoon canola oil

1/2 cup light sour cream, plus extra for garnish

Salt and Pepper to taste

1 cup diced cilantro leaves

Directions: Place in a slow cooker the following: the sweet potato chunks, onion, garlic, chipotle pepper, smoked paprika, cumin, vegetable broth, vinegar and soy sauce. Cook on high for 3 to 4 hours or on low for 6 to 8 hours.

Whisk the sour cream and some salt and pepper to taste into the soup in slow cooker. Blend in batches in your blender or blend with a stick blender until smooth. Spoon into serving bowls. Top with a little sour cream drizzled, cilantro.

Barbecued Sweet Potatoes
Ingredients:
1 lb. sweet potatoes, cut lengthwise into ¼" slices
1 Tablespoon of Worcestershire sauce
1 Tablespoon of red wine vinegar
3 Tablespoons of ketchup
1 teaspoon of chili chipotle powder
1/2 teaspoon of black pepper

Directions: Set the grill the medium-hot fire/heat; spray
grill rack with nonstick cooking spray.
In a large bowl, combine all ingredients except the
potatoes. Mix well. Add potato slices into bowl, and toss
well, making sure to coat each potato slice thoroughly with
the sauce.
Grill potatoes, turning often, and brushing with sauce ,
until browned and crispy on the outside, but tender on the
inside – about 10 minutes.

Swiss Chard

Swiss Chard is, in my opinion, one of the most beautiful
vegetables out there. It's large green leaves are nothing
new when you're surrounded by spinach, lettuce and kale.
But the stems! Oh those gorgeous stems! Vibrant shades of
pink, orange, yellow and burgundy red. It's a surprise
every time I go out to cut some. Swiss chard is close to
spinach in it's nutrients and a great plant to grow because
it's a "cut and come again" type of plant that we can
harvest all spring and fall. One of my favorite uses of swiss
chard is to take the stems and use them as if they were
celery. They have that same crunch and shape and are
great on a veggie tray or diced up in a pasta, chicken or
tuna salad. You can enjoy the leaves much like spinach,
however the leaves are a bit more intense.

Storing Swiss Chard: Don't wash your chard until you're ready to use it. Just wrap tightly in a bag and store in your crisper drawer. It should last a week or so.

Preserving Swiss Chard: Like most other greens you can blanch the leaves and freeze for future use. Just wash the leaves and place in a pot of boiling water for 1 minute. Remove and immediately submerge into an bowl of ice water. Drain and pack into freezer bags. Add frozen chard in soups, sauces or just sauté with oil and garlic for a nice side dish.

Baked Swiss Chard Stems with Olive Oil and Parmesan
Ingredients:
1 bunch chard stems
1/2 teaspoon of salt
olive oil for spraying pan and chard
1/2 cup coarsely grated parmesan cheese coarse ground black pepper to taste

Directions: Trim the rough ends from chard stems, then cut stems on an angle into pieces about 3 inches long. If some stems are very thick, you may wish to cut them lengthwise so all pieces are approximately the same thickness.

Preheat oven to 400 F. Bring a pot of water to a boil, add salt and chard stems and boil about 6 minutes. Let chard drain well.

Drizzle oil in a non-stick baking. Place chard in the pan and lightly drizzle with more olive oil, then sprinkle with cheese. Make two layers, drizzling each layer with oil and sprinkling with cheese. Bake about 20 minutes, or until chard is softened and cheese is slightly browned on the edges. Season with fresh ground black pepper if desired and serve hot.

Creamed Swiss Chard

Ingredients:
2 bunches of Swiss chard,
3 or 4 slices bacon, diced
1 clove garlic, finely minced
1/4 to 1/2 cup finely chopped red onion
2 Tablespoons butter
2 Tablespoons flour
1 cup half-and-half or whole milk
pinch nutmeg
salt and pepper, to taste

Directions: Wash chard and cut off thicker stems. Thinly slice the stems and chop leaves into 1/2- to 1-inch pieces. Steam or boil the stems for about 5 minutes, then add chard and cook until wilted, about 4 minutes longer. Drain well, squeezing out excess moisture if necessary.

In a medium saucepan over medium heat, cook the diced bacon until crisp; remove and set aside. Add onion and garlic and cook until onion is tender. Stir in the cooked, drained chard and the reserved bacon; set aside.

In a saucepan over medium heat, melt butter. Stir in the flour until smooth and bubbly. Add the half-and-half or milk and nutmeg. Cook, stirring, until smooth and thickened. Add salt and pepper, to taste.

Add about 1/2 of the sauce to the chard, stirring to blend. Stir in more or all of the remaining sauce mixture, as desired.

Skillet Macaroni with Swiss Chard

Ingredients:

1 Tablespoon of olive oil

10-12 Swiss chard leaves, chopped

2 cups spaghetti sauce

1 teaspoon of Italian seasonings (oregano, basil, thyme)

12 oz. elbow macaroni noodles

2 cups water, or beef broth

1/2 cup Parmesan cheese

Directions: Add the olive oil to a 12 inch deep dish skillet and sauté the chopped Swiss chard leaves for 2-3 minutes, or until bright green and soft.

Stir in the spaghetti sauce and Italian seasonings. Stir in 2 cups of hot water (or beef broth), along with the pasta noodles. Gently combine so the pasta noodles are under the liquid. Add more liquid, 1/4 cup at a time, until all the pasta is under the liquid.

Bring to bubbling, then cover tightly and cook over medium heat for 8- 10 minutes, stirring once.

Once the pasta is al dente, remove the skillet from the heat and uncover. Let sit for a few minutes and let the sauce thicken if necessary. Toss in the Parmesan cheese and stir. Serve hot.

Stuffed Swiss Chard Leaves

Ingredients:

1 cup of brown rice (cooked and cooled)

15 swiss chard leaves

1 1/2 pounds ground beef

1/2 medium onion

3 Tablespoons of olive oil

several cloves of garlic, minced

2 eggs, lightly beaten

3 tomatoes, peeled, seeded and diced

6 mushrooms, sliced

1/4 cup parsley, minced

salt, pepper

Topping:

either a tomato sauce OR a mixture of:

1/4 cup bread crumbs

1/4 parmesan cheese

1/2 teaspoon of dried basil

Directions: Start by bringing a large pot of water to boil. Cut off the stalks of the swiss chard and cook them in the boiling water for about two or three minutes. The point is to make them pliable enough to stuff easily. Drain and run cold water over the leaves to stop the cooking and to make them easier to work with.

Sauté the chopped onion in the olive oil until translucent, then add the meat and sauté until cooked through. Drain off any remaining water or oil and put into a large bowl. Sauté the mushrooms and garlic until cooked, then add them to the bowl, along with the diced tomatoes, parsley and salt and pepper to taste. Add the cooled rice to the bowl, then the beaten eggs and mix everything well.

Dry the swiss chard leaves a little, and lay them out on a counter top. Place about 1/4 cup of stuffing on each leaf, then start rolling up the leaves from the stalk end, folding in the sides as you roll. Place in a greased casserole. Top with either a tomato sauce or a mixture of bread crumbs, parmesan cheese and herbs. Bake in preheated 375 degree oven for about 1/2 hour.

T

Tomatillos

If I'm ever at a Mexican restaurant and I see the words "Salsa Verde" then I am a happy girl. I don't know what it is about these little green fruits (yes, they are actually fruit!) that bring such joy to my life. Maybe it's that they come wrapped in a cute little brown "package" or possibly it's the twang of citrusy, tomato flavor that just ZINGS on my tongue. I don't know what it is... but boy do I like it. Tomatillos are in the tomato family but they are NOT tomatoes. They deserve the recognition of being their own fruit!

Storing tomatillos: Unlike tomatoes, you do want to store your tomatillos in the refrigerator. Store in a paper bag and they will last about a week. They will last even longer with their husks removed. Ahhh! Naked tomatillos!

Preserving tomatillos: I prefer to make Salsa Verde but that's because I LOVE it. You can also just freeze them. Remove the husks, gently wash and dry and pop into a freezer bag. Done!

Alright... enough talk. Here is a the salsa verde recipe I hold close to my heart:

Salsa Verde

Ingredients:

8 tomatillos, husks removed, tomatillos chopped

1/2 white onion, diced

1 bunch of cilantro, chopped

1 jalapeno pepper, chopped (use a Serrano for more heat)

1 lime, juiced

2 cloves of garlic

3 Tablespoons of orange juice

1 teaspoon of salt

1 teaspoon of black pepper

Directions: Chop ingredients. Add all ingredients to blender. LEAVE OUT a Tablespoon of chopped onion and a pinch of cilantro. Blend well until salsa becomes smooth. Do not over blend. If the salsa is too thick, add more orange juice. Pour salsa into a serving bowl. Stir in excess onions and top with cilantro garnish. Salt and pepper to taste.

Hide in the back of the refrigerator like I have to or else your husband (or kids, neighbors, third-cousin on your mama's side, etc.) will eat it all.

Tomatillo, Cilantro and Lime Butter

Sounds crazy, I know... but try it slathered on some grilled corn on the cob. Then you'll think I'm the smartest girl in the world!

Ingredients:

1 tomatillo, husk removed, and chopped

2 Tablespoons chopped cilantro

1 teaspoon lime zest (about 1 small lime)

1 teaspoon chopped fresh garlic

½ to 1 teaspoon finely chopped jalapeño pepper

½ teaspoon salt

8 tablespoons (1 stick) unsalted butter, softened

Directions: Place the tomatillo, cilantro, lime zest, garlic, jalapeño pepper, and salt in a food processor and thoroughly combine. Add the butter and combine until just blended.

Scoop the flavored butter onto a piece of waxed paper and roll into a cylindrical shape. Refrigerate for at least 1 hour. Also really good mixed with pasta or on cornbread!

Chickpea and Tomatillo Soup

Ingredients:

4 cups (about 3 14-oz cans) chickpeas, rinsed if canned
1 cup tomatillos, pureed
3 tomatillos, chopped
3 cups chicken or vegetable stock
5 cloves of garlic, coarsely chopped
2 medium onions, thinly sliced
1/4 cup olive oil
Pinch of chili powder
1 bunch of cilantro, chopped
Salt

Directions: Heat oil in a large saucepan over a medium flame. Add onions and sauté, stirring occasionally, until soft. Add chopped garlic and stir for about one minute. Add tomatillo puree, chickpeas, chopped tomatillos and stock.

Bring mixture to a simmer and cover, simmering for 20 minutes. Add chili powder and salt to taste. Just before serving, stir in chopped cilantro.

Roasted Tomatillo and Chicken Pasta

Ingredients:

1/2 lb. tomatillos (about 4 medium-sized tomatillos)

6 cloves garlic

1 Tablespoon of olive oil

4 cups of fresh baby spinach

1 cup of fresh basil

2 Tablespoons of chicken broth

2 Tablespoons of fresh oregano (2 teaspoons dried)

2 Tablespoon of fresh thyme (2 teaspoons dried)

1 Tablespoon of sugar

1 teaspoon of salt

1 teaspoon of red pepper flakes

½ cups of. grated Parmesan cheese

12 oz. dry pasta (I like penne or rigatoni)

1 large chicken breast cooked and shredded

½ cup of Parmesan cheese

1 cup of mozzarella cheese

Directions: Preheat oven to 400 degrees. Remove husks from tomatillos and quarter. Place tomatillos and garlic in a bowl; add oil and toss to coat ingredients. Spread tomatillos and garlic cloves in a baking pan and roast for 35 minutes. Place roasted tomatillos mixture in a food processor; add spinach, basil, broth, oregano, thyme, sugar, salt, pepper, and parmesan cheese. Process until sauce in blended.

Cook pasta according to package instructions. Drain and set aside. Mix pasta, tomatillo sauce, chicken and Parmesan cheese and put into a 9x13 baking dish. Top with mozzarella cheese and bake at 350 degrees for 30 minutes.

Tomatillo Bread Salad

Ingredients:

3 slices stale bread, cubed

1 teaspoon cumin

1 teaspoon cayenne

1 teaspoon ground oregano

4 tomatillos, husk removed, cleaned and roasted

2 small onions, thinly sliced

1 cup black beans, rinsed

1 Tablespoon olive oil

Juice from one lime

Salt and pepper to taste

Cilantro, finely chopped

Directions: Toss bread cubes with herbs and spices and oil. Toast in a 400 degree oven for about 8 minutes, stirring occasionally to brown evenly. Roughly chop roasted tomatillos, reserving any juice that they release. Toss together tomatillos, onions, bread and beans. Drizzle with tomatillo juice and lime juice, season with salt and pepper and serve at room temperature, garnished with cilantro

Tomatoes

I know very few people that are at a lost for tomato recipes. When the tomatoes first come in season most people are quite content slicing them up and eating them. At least I sure am. But what happens when you grow tired of tomatoes (blasphemy!) or you have too many and you don't know what to do with all of them! Maybe you just need some tomato inspiration and that's where I come in. I am a lover of all things tomatoes. If it was socially acceptable, I'd take a bath in tomatoes every day! (Well, not really....) As a child I have clear memories of my Grandpa Harold coming in for lunch from farming and eating sliced tomatoes with a sprinkle of salt. Tomatoes embody everything that is good and pure. Long live the tomato!

Storing tomatoes: Contrary to popular belief, you do not need to store your tomatoes in the fridge. In fact it's actually a bad idea. Refrigerating tomatoes makes them mushy and zaps the flavor. Just store them, unwashed, on your counter until you're ready to use them.

Preserving tomatoes: Shoot... I could write a book just on this subject. There are very few things that trump eating your owned canned tomatoes. But I also love to freeze mine. Or even dry them! Here's the scoop: I can whole tomatoes for things like chili or soup. Or I'll can salsa. I follow the Ball Blue Book instructions that are out on the web or in their "Blue Book." Canning is something you need to do some reading on so I'm not going to go into great depth here. However it's not a difficult thing to do, you just need to get trustworthy directions (Ball Blue Book, or another book called "It's So Easy to Preserve" or your local extension's website) and follow those directions exactly.

When it comes to freezing, sometimes I'll freeze tomatoes whole. Then I just run the frozen tomato under hot water and the skin peels right off! It's amazing!

Garden Spaghetti Sauce

Ingredients:

6 pounds of tomatoes, peeled and cored

2 cloves of garlic, minced

1 onion. Diced

1 teaspoon of salt

1 teaspoon of pepper

1 teaspoon of sugar

1 teaspoon of dried oregano

2 bay leaves

¼ teaspoon of red pepper flakes

Directions: To peel the tomatoes: place in boiling water for one minute and then transfer to a bowl of ice-cold water for one minute. Run your knife gently along the tomato to pierce the skin and then peel. It should peel off very easily! Place tomatoes (chop after peeling and cutting out the core and any blemishes), onion, garlic, oregano, salt, pepper and red pepper into a deep sauce pan or sauté pan. Bring to boil and cook on medium heat for 2 hours . Stir occasionally.

Remove from heat and puree in a food processor or blender. Pour mixture back into pan and add bay leaves. Let sit for 30 minutes so sauce can absorb the bay leaf flavor. Then remove bay leaf and spoon into quart sized freezer bags or another freezer safe container. (if canning, leave one inch head space and process in a hot water bath for 35 minutes).

Tomato Pie

My Aunt Laura and Aunt Maria LOVE this stuff! Thanks for the recipe guys!

Ingredients:

4 large tomatoes, peeled and sliced

1/2 cup chopped fresh basil

2 onions sliced thin

Oregano to taste

6-10 slices of bacon, cooked and crumbled (optional)

2 cups shredded Mozzarella cheese

1/4 cup mayonnaise

One prepared frozen pie crust

Directions: Preheat oven to 375 degrees F.

In alternating layers, fill pastry shell with tomatoes, basil, onions, bacon, garlic oregano In a small bowl, mix cheese with mayonnaise. Spread mixture over top of pie. Cover loosely with aluminum foil.

Bake in preheated oven for 30 minutes. Remove foil from top of pie and bake an additional 30 minutes. Serve warm or cold.

Panzanella (Tuscan Bread and Tomato Salad)

Ingredients:

3 Tablespoons olive oil

1 small French bread 1-inch cubes (6 cups)

1 teaspoon salt

2 large, ripe tomatoes, cut into 1-inch cubes

1 cucumber, unpeeled, seeded, and sliced 1/2-inch thick

1 red bell pepper, seeded and cut into 1-inch cubes

1 yellow bell pepper, seeded and cut into 1-inch cubes

1/2 red onion, cut in 1/2 and thinly sliced

20 large basil leaves, coarsely chopped

For the vinaigrette:

1 teaspoon finely minced garlic

1/2 teaspoon Dijon mustard

3 tablespoons Champagne vinegar (I've also used red wine vinegar and it's amazing!)

1/2 cup olive oil

1/2 teaspoon salt

1/4 teaspoon ground black pepper

Directions: Heat the oil in a large saute pan. Add the bread and salt; cook over low to medium heat, tossing frequently, for 10 minutes, or until nicely browned. Add more oil as needed.

For the vinaigrette, whisk all the ingredients together. In a large bowl, mix the tomatoes, cucumber, red pepper, yellow pepper, red onion, and basil. Add the bread cubes and toss with the vinaigrette. Season liberally with salt and pepper. Serve, or allow the salad to sit for about half an hour for the flavors to blend.

Tomato Basil Sandwiches

Ahh.. my favorite summer treat!

Ingredients:

8 slices of ciabatta bread (I've also used focaccia or a yummy sourdough)

8 slices of tomato (heirlooms are great for this)

4 slices of fresh mozzarella

4 basil leaves

olive oil

salt and pepper

Directions: Toast bread either in the oven or on the grill. Drizzle toasted bread with olive oil. Add tomato, basil and cheese. Sprinkle with salt and pepper. Makes 4 sandwiches.

Garden Gazpacho

A soup that uses up lots of summer veggies & keeps the kitchen cool!

Ingredients:

2 cups tomato juice

1.5 pounds tomatoes, peeled, seeded, and chopped

1 cup chicken or vegetable stock

1 Tablespoons of olive oil

1 Tablespoons of red wine vinegar

2 cloves garlic, minced

2 small cucumbers, peeled and chopped

1/4 cup red onion, chopped

1/4 cup fresh basil, chopped

1/2 red bell pepper, chopped

1/2 yellow bell pepper, chopped

Salt and pepper

Directions: In a large bowl, stir all ingredients together. Reserve 1 cup from this and transfer the rest to a blender or food processor and process until smooth. Stir in reserved cup of soup and add salt, pepper to taste. Chill for at least an hour or overnight; serve cold with a dollop of sour cream and croutons or crusty bread.

Pico de Gallo
Ingredients:
2 cups ripe red tomatoes diced (about 4 medium tomatoes)
1/4 cup diced onion (about 1/4 of a small white onion)
1/4 cup chopped cilantro
1 jalapenos (stem and seeds removed) diced
1 lime, juiced
Salt to taste

Directions: Mix all the ingredients and let it sit for half an hour.

Caprese Salad
One afternoon on the farm I made a HUGE lunch that included this salad. I forgot to serve it and consequently it sat in the fridge until the next day. I'm so very glad I forgot the salad because the sitting time allowed the flavors to really meld together. If you can, make this ahead of time!
Ingredients:
4 tomatoes, sliced
1 ball of fresh mozzarella, sliced
Extra virgin olive oil
Salt
Pepper
Balsamic vinegar
a bunch of basil, cut into thin strips (see note)

Directions: Simply slice tomatoes and mozzarella and arrange in a circular pattern on a plate. Sprinkle with basil ribbons. Drizzle with olive oil, salt, pepper and balsamic vinegar. Lightly cover and chill over night.

To cut the basil: The easiest method is a "chiffonade." Basically, you stack your basil leaves on top of each other and roll tightly like a cigar (not that I've ever rolled a cigar but I got the point, and I'm sure you will too). Simply take your sharp knife and cut across the rolled leaves. Then you will have small ribbons of basil. Brilliant!

Turnips

Turnips, like rutabagas, get a bad rap for being peasant food. Well those peasants knew a good thing when they saw one! Turnips are a great staple crop that can be used in many different ways and offers health benefits like potassium and vitamin C. Turnip greens, the leafy tops of a turnip plant, are also an excellent source of nutrition. We like to eat turnips raw and cooked so get creative if you find yourself with an abundance! Turnips are also great because they last a long time if stored properly!

Storing Turnips: If your turnips still have their greens attached, remove the greens when you get them home. Clean, store, and cook the greens as you would spinach or chard. Store turnips loosely wrapped in a plastic bag in the crisper of the fridge. Like any root vegetable, they want a cool, dark, dry environment.

Preserving Turnips: Luckily turnips have a long shelf life in the fridge but you can also freeze them for use in soups. I also came across a really interesting version of Lebanese Pickled Turnips. Apparently, this is the ONLY way to pickle turnips! (not really, but these are the best turnips I've ever had and I don't even like beets!)

Lebanese Pickled Turnips

Ingredients:

5 medium turnips

1 small beet

2 cups water

1 cup white vinegar

1 Tablespoon of salt

1 Tablespoon of sugar

4 cloves garlic, peeled

2 dried chiles

Directions: First get your brine going. Add the water, vinegar, salt and sugar to a saucepan and boil. Remove from heat after a minute or two, and set aside.

Wash the veggies, cut off the ends and peel. Cut the turnips and beets wedges. Drop two wedges of beets into the bottom of two sterilized quart jars. Toss a couple garlic cloves in each was well as one chile per jar. Pack in the turnips fairly tightly, and pour the hot brine over to cover. You may need a little more, just quickly bring water and vinegar in a 2:1 ratio up to a boil and add.

Seal up the jars, and leave to cool before refrigerating. These aren't hot water canned, so you've got to keep them cold, no storing in the pantry for later use unless you're a big fan of taking your chances with botulism.

You'll see things turning pink right away, but for best flavor and color give them a couple days.

Swiss Turnip Gratin

Adapted from the Pioneer Woman's version

Ingredients:

4 whole Turnips

4 cloves Garlic

2 cups shredded swiss cheese (or you can use cheddar if you don't feel like buying a brick of swiss and grating it yourself).

4 Tablespoons of butter

Chicken Broth

Heavy Cream

Salt And Pepper, to taste

Fresh Herbs, to taste

Directions: Preheat the oven to 375°. Start by peeling and thinly slicing the turnips and mincing the cloves of garlic. Grate about 2 cups of cheese.

In a large oven-proof skillet, melt 2-3 tablespoons of butter over medium-low heat. Place a single layer of turnips on top of the butter.

Sprinkle a little of the garlic on top, then add a couple of tablespoons of butter.

Drizzle a healthy splash of chicken broth over the turnips. Next, do the same with the cream. Now add a nice layer of cheese – about ½ cup. Sprinkle a bit of salt.

Repeat these layers twice more. Sprinkle on some freshly ground black pepper.

Now pop the whole thing into the over and bake for about 20 minutes or until the top is hot, brown and bubbly.

Spicy White Bean and Turnip Soup

This recipe uses dry beans, which is a much cheaper route. However, if you want to use canned beans just use 2 cups of rinsed beans.

Ingredients:

1 1/2 cups dried cannellini (white kidney) beans
5 cups water
1 bay leaf
2 Tablespoons olive oil
1 large onion, chopped
3 garlic cloves, minced or crushed
2 medium turnips, peeled and chopped
1 large potato, diced
1 large carrot, chopped
1 red bell pepper, chopped
1 teaspoon hot paprika
1/2 teaspoon dried red pepper flakes, or to taste
1 teaspoon salt, or to taste
fresh ground black pepper
small handful fresh parsley, finely chopped

Directions: Rinse the beans under running water and soak overnight covered in several inches of cold water. Drain the following day and add to a large saucepan along with 5 cups of fresh water and a bay leaf. Bring to a boil, then reduce heat to low, cover, and simmer for 1 hour or until the beans are just tender. Remove from heat and set aside.

Heat a large saucepan or soup pot over medium heat. Add olive oil. Add the onion and cook for 5 minutes or until the onion turns translucent. Add the garlic, turnips, potato and carrots, and sauté for 1 minute. Stir in the red pepper, paprika, chili flakes, along with the beans and their cooking liquid.

Bring the soup to a boil, then reduce the heat to low, cover, and simmer for 20 to 30 minutes or until the vegetables are tender.

Take off of heat and remove the bay leaf. Season with salt and black pepper to taste. Sprinkle chopped parsley for garnish.

Turnip Chips
Ingredients:
3 medium turnips sliced thin
1/4 teaspoon of chili powder
1/4 teaspoon of garlic powder
1/4 teaspoon of onion powder
salt to taste
1 1/2 - 2 Tablespoons of olive oil

Directions: Preheat the oven to 350 Cover a baking sheet with foil. Slice the turnips thin, the thinner they are the crispier they will be.

Put the slices in a large mixing bowl and add the olive oil. Mix well to coat all the pieces. In a small bowl combine the spices. Then add to the larger bowl and mix to evenly. Put the slices on the baking sheet and bake for 30-50 minutes flipping every 10 minutes or so. Remove from the oven when they look crisp enough for your liking. Make sure to go easy on the olive oil so they don't get too soggy.

Winter Root Vegetable Soup
Sally McDaniel of Sally's Fields (She's one awesome
farmer!)

I haphazardly decided to put this recipe under turnips,
although it uses lots of different types of winter vegetables
and could be categorized under any of them. I figured most
folks need more ideas for what to do with turnips! If you're
missing some of the veggies just substitute (for instance,
no parsnips, use more carrots, etc).

Ingredients:
3 or 4 garlic cloves
3 parsnips, peeled and chopped
3 carrots, peeled and chopped
1 celery root, peeled and chopped
2 turnips, chopped
1 sweet potato, peeled and chopped
1 butternut squash, peeled and chopped
1/4 cup olive oil
1 teaspoon kosher salt
1/2 teaspoon ground black pepper
3 tablespoons butter
1 stalk celery, diced
1/2 sweet onion, diced
1 quart vegetable broth (or any broth-based soup stock)
1/2 cup half-and-half cream
salt and ground black pepper to taste

Directions: Combine parsnips, carrots, celery root, turnips,
sweet potato, and butternut squash in a large roasting pan.
Drizzle with olive oil, and season with 1 teaspoon of kosher
salt and 1/2 teaspoon of pepper. Toss vegetables to evenly
distribute seasonings.

Roast in a 425 degree oven until the vegetables are easily

pierced with a fork and skins are browned, 30 to 45 minutes, stirring regularly. (Don't skip this step! It adds delicious deep roasted flavor to the final soup.)
Meanwhile, melt the butter in a large pot or Dutch oven over medium heat. Stir in the garlic, celery, and onion; cook and stir until the onion has softened and turned translucent, about 5 minutes. Pour in the vegetable broth and bring to a simmer, uncovered.
Stir in the roasted vegetables and continue simmering for 10 minutes. Puree the soup, using an immersion blender. (Or in a food processor or blender, in batches.)
Stir in the half and half, and season with salt and pepper, if necessary. If the soup becomes too thick, add more vegetable broth.

Honey-Thyme Roasted Turnips, Carrots and Mushrooms
Ingredients:
4-5 medium sized turnips, scrubbed clean
4 carrots, peeled
1 cup thickly-sliced shitake mushrooms
3 sprigs fresh thyme
1/4 cup plus 2 Tablespoons olive oil
2 Tablespoons honey
1 Tablespoon balsamic vinegar
salt & pepper

Directions: Preheat oven to 400 degrees. Chop turnips and carrots into 1/2-inch pieces. In a large bowl, toss turnip and carrot pieces with 1/4 cup olive oil, making sure to evenly coat vegetables. Season with salt and pepper, and pour onto a baking sheet . Tuck thyme in between the vegetables. Roast for 20 minutes, until bottom sides are beginning to brown.

Remove from oven, add honey and balsamic vinegar and stir. Sprinkle mushrooms across top, and drizzle with additional 2 tablespoons of olive oil. Add a little more salt, return to oven and roast an additional 20-25 minutes. Turnips should be easily pierced with a fork when it's done.

Winter Squash

Last year our winter squash plants shriveled up and died before we got any squash. I went through all 7 of the stages of grief in about 30 minutes. Then bought some from another local farmer. I can't go an entire year without homemade butternut squash soup. It's just impossible. Most of the winter squash recipes are interchangeable. So if the recipe calls for butternut and you've got Hubbard squash, I say give it a go. Types of winter squash: pumpkin, butternut, acorn, hubbard, spaghetti, turban, kobacha, etc!

Storing Winter Squash: Winter squash will last for months if kept in a cool, dry place. I still have a couple butternut squash that I bought 5 months ago. They look and feel perfect. Hubbard squashes will last even longer.
Preserving squash: A great way to save some of your winter squash for later is to just store it well. But you can freeze it or can it. The latter involves a pressure cooker to process the jars. Don't try to use the water bath method as the temperatures don't get high enough to kill botulism-causing organisms.

Some folks don't know the basics of roasting winter squash... so here's the general method:

Cut the squashes in half and scooped out the stringy pulp and seeds inside. Drizzle cut-side of squash with olive oil. Place all the squash on a foil lined baking sheet, cut side down. Bake in a 400 degree oven for 1 hr or until the squash is tender (like a potato).

Classic Butternut Squash Soup

I made this for our first ever CSA meeting and I didn't take any home. So I think that's a good sign. Put a tablespoon of cream in each bowl to make it really rich and decadent. You can also make this vegetarian/vegan by using vegetable stock instead of chicken stock. This soup freezes like a pro and is a great go to dinner when all you've got time to do is defrost it and re-heat on the stove.

Ingredients:
2 Tablespoons olive oil
2/3 cup diced carrot (about 1 large carrot)
1/2 cup diced celery (about 1 large stalk)
2/3 cup diced onion (about 1 medium onion)
4 cups cubed butternut squash (about 1 medium squash)
1/2 teaspoon chopped fresh thyme
4 to 6 cups low-sodium chicken broth
salt and ground black pepper, to taste

Directions: Heat olive oil in a large soup pot. Add carrot, celery and onion. Cook until vegetables have begun to soften and onion turns translucent, 3 to 4 minutes. Add butternut squash and thyme. Stir to combine with vegetables. Stir in chicken broth and season with salt and pepper.
Bring to a boil, reduce heat and simmer until squash is fork-tender, about 30 minutes. Use an immersion blender to puree soup. Alternatively, let the soup cool slightly and carefully puree in batches in a traditional blender or use a food mill.

Butternut Squash Fries

Ingredients:

1 Butternut Squash

Salt (coarse sea salt or a flaky salt works best)

Olive oil

Directions: Preheat oven to 425 degrees. Peel the squash and slice in half. Remove the seeds. Cut up into strips similar to french fries. Place on a cookie sheet that's been sprayed with a non-stick spray or take some olive oil and wipe it around the plan with a towel. Mist some olive oil over the squash and sprinkle with salt. Bake at 40 flipping halfway through. The fries are done when they are starting to turn brown on the edges and get crispy. Great served with maple syrup rather than ketchup!

Herbed Spaghetti Squash

Ingredients:

1 small spaghetti squash,

2 1/2 Tablespoons butter

2 1/2 Tablespoons herbs, such as basil, chives, dill, parsley and sage

1/2 teaspoon salt

1/8 teaspoon freshly ground black pepper

Directions: Preheat the oven to 375 degrees F. Using a sharp knife, cut the squash in half lengthwise and place, cut side down, in a baking dish. Add enough water to come 1/2-inch up the sides of the baking dish and cover with aluminum foil. Bake for 45 minutes, until the squash is easily pierced with a paring knife. Remove from the oven, uncover, and allow to cool slightly. Using a spoon, remove the seeds and discard. Using a fork, gently pull the strands of squash away from the peel and place the squash strands into a mixing bowl. Finely chop the herbs and set aside. Heat a skillet. Add the butter, spaghetti squash, herbs, salt and pepper and toss thoroughly but gently to heat and combine. Serve immediately or cover and keep warm until ready to serve.

Roasted Corn Pudding in Acorn Squash

Adapted from www.101cookbooks.com

I used an acorn squash here, but you can experiment with other types of squash if you like.

Ingredients:

1 small (2 lb.) acorn squash, cut in half lengthwise and seeded

1 Tablespoon olive oil

1 cup milk

1 egg plus 2 egg whites

1/2 cup fresh corn kernels (or more if you like)

1/2 cup chopped scallions

a tiny pinch of freshly grated nutmeg

1/4 teaspoon fine grain sea salt

1/3 cup grated white cheddar cheese

Directions: Preheat the oven to 375F degrees with a rack in the middle. Rub the orange flesh of the squash with the oil. Place cut side up on a baking sheet. You will want it to sit flat (and not tip), if you are having trouble just level out the bottom using a knife. If the squash is tilting on the pan, the filling will run out - bad news. Cover the squash with foil and bake for 40 minutes or until the squash starts to get tender.

In a bowl combine the milk, eggs, corn, half of the scallions, nutmeg, and salt. Fill each of the squash bowls 3/4 full (see head notes about using leftovers). Carefully transfer the squash back to the oven without spilling (tricky!). Continue baking uncovered for another 30 - 50 minutes, or until the squash is fully cooked through, and the pudding has set. The amount of time it takes can vary wildly depending on the squash and oven. At the last minute sprinkle with cheese and finish with a flash under the broiler to brown the cheese. Keep an eye on things, you can go from melted cheese to burnt and inedible in a flash. Serve hot sprinkled with the remaining scallions.

Butternut Squash Risotto

I've had this in a few restaurants, and every time I thought "I've got to make this at home!" Here's the closest thing I could find to heaven.

Ingredients:

4 cups chicken broth

2 cups cream of butternut squash soup

1/2 cup white wine

5 Tablespoons of butter

2 strips of apple smoked bacon, diced

1/2 cup white onion diced

1 1/2 cups of butternut squash cubed

Olive oil

1 1/2 cup Arborio rice

1 cup freshly grated Parmesan cheese

2 teaspoon salt

1 teaspoon pepper

Directions: Preheat oven to 400 degrees. Coat the cubed butternut squash with olive oil and 1 teaspoon salt. Roast on a baking sheet for 20 minutes. In a medium sauce pan over a medium heat pour chicken broth and cream of butternut squash soup and simmer for 10 minutes. In a large pot, melt butter. Once butter is melted throw in diced bacon and diced onions. Saute in butter for a few minutes until onions are translucent. Next, pour in dry Arborio rice and stir until rice is coated (stir for about two minutes). Pour white wine over the rice mixture; stir for another two minutes over a medium heat

Then, begin by pouring soup mixture one to two cups at a time. Toss in 1 teaspoon of salt, and 1 teaspoon of pepper.

Stir rice until mixture begins to look absorbed. Pour another one to two cups of soup into mixture and stir until absorbed. Repeat until all of the soup is gone and rice looks creamy. Remove from stove and stir in roasted butternut squash and Parmesan. Enjoy hot.

Kabocha Squash with Sage and Leeks
Ingredients:
1 large kabocha squash
Olive oil
1 Tablespoon salt, plus more to taste
2 leeks, washed, bulb and greens removed
1/2 pound unsalted butter
4 Tablespoons fresh sage leaves
1/2 teaspoon black pepper

Directions: Preheat the oven to 350 degrees.
Rub the squash generously with olive oil and season well with salt. Pierce 3 holes in the top of the squash with a sharp object to allow the steam to vent when cooking. Place on a baking sheet and roast for about 1 hour, or until thoroughly soft and easily pierced with a fork. Remove from the oven.
When cool enough to handle, cut open the squash, carefully remove the seeds and throw away. Using a large spoon, scoop out all of the flesh and place in a bowl or container, Throw away the skin (compost!).

Cut the leeks lengthwise and julienne into straw-like strips, about 2 inches in length, and set aside.

Heat the butter over medium heat in a large saucepan and cook until the color reaches brown-butter stage. Add the fresh sage leaves and continue cooking until the sage becomes slightly crisped. Add the julienne of leeks and continue stirring until cooked, about 2 minutes. Add the 1

Tablespoon of salt and ½ teaspoon of pepper and stir to blend.

Add the cooked squash and continue to stir over medium heat to mash the squash and to blend all of the ingredients together. (Some large pieces of squash may remain, or they can be mashed with a back of a spoon if a smoother consistency is desired.)

Spoon the squash into a large serving bowl and serve.

Z

Zucchini

Vegetables are a must on a diet. I suggest carrot cake, zucchini bread, and pumpkin pie." - Jim Davis, 'Garfield'

Honestly, it's hard to come up with something thought-provoking or witty to say about zucchini. Furthermore I have no interesting stories about zucchini. It's just there. It's not that it isn't inspiring. We grow it. It's reliable. We like to eat it. It's just that I've made it all the way to Z and I'm hungry from typing all these recipes and I'm ready to stop typing and start cooking. Hmph!

I do know the smaller than zuch the more tender and awesome it tastes. The big ones are still great, make bread or cake!

Storing Zucchini: No need to refrigerate your zuchs! Just store them on the counter away from direct heat.
Preserving Zucchini: I find the best way is to freeze it. But the key is to prep it as if you were using the zucchini right

then. For instance, if I want to preserve zucchini to make bread or cake at a later time I will shred the zucchini in my food processor or my box grater first. Then I let it drain a bit in a colander before I pack it into freezer bags. Or maybe I want to preserve it for soups. Then I'll dice it and bag it up. Don't worry about blanching it!

Grilled Zucchini

Ingredients:

4 medium zucchini cut into 1/4-inch-thick sliced, longwise

2 clove garlic, minced

1/4 cup olive oil salt and pepper

Directions: If using a gas grill, preheat it to high. If using a charcoal grill, pile the coals together to create a hot zone for direct grilling. Oil the grill by holding a folded wad of paper towel with tongs, dipping it in vegetable oil, and brushing the oil (sparingly -- it's flammable) onto the grill grate.

Rinse and dry the zucchini. Cut off the ends and discard them. Cut the zucchini lengthwise into 1/4-inch-thick planks. Put the zucchini planks in a large bowl and toss with the garlic and olive oil, and sprinkle with salt and pepper. Grill the zucchini over direct heat until they're well browned, 4-6 minutes per side.

Minestrone Soup

For a vegetarian version, replace the chicken stock with vegetable broth

Ingredients:

2 Tablespoons extra-virgin olive oil

1 pound zucchini, diced

2 ribs celery, finely chopped

1 small carrot, finely chopped

1 onion, finely chopped

1 bay leaf

3 cloves garlic, minced

salt and pepper to taste

4 cups of chicken stock

15oz can cannellini beans, rinsed

15oz can crushed tomatoes (I usually just use a quart of my homemade tomato sauce).

¼ pound of pasta (small shells, macaroni noodles, etc.)

1 teaspoon of dried thyme

1 teaspoon of dried oregano

½ teaspoon of freshly ground pepper

Salt to taste

Directions: In a soup pot, heat the oil over medium-high heat. Add the zucchini, celery, carrot, onion, and 2 cloves garlic; season with salt and pepper. Cook until the vegetables are tender, 7 to 8 minutes.

Stir in the stock, beans and tomatoes and bring it to a boil. Add thyme, oregano and bay leaf. Add the pasta and cook until al dente. When ready to serve fish out the bay leave. Serve warm with crusty bread and some freshly grated parmesan cheese on top.

Chocolate Zucchini Cake

Super moist and you'll have no leftovers... I promise!

Ingredients:

1/2 cup butter at room temperature

1/2 cup vegetable oil1

3/4 cups granulated sugar

1 teaspoon vanilla

1 teaspoon baking soda

1/2 teaspoon baking powder

1/2 teaspoon salt

2 large eggs

1/2 cup yogurt

2 1/2 cups unbleached all-purpose flour

3/4 cup Dutch-process cocoa

2 cups shredded zucchini (about one 10" zucchini)

1/2 cup chocolate chips

For the frosting:

6 oz heavy cream

1 bag of semi-sweet chocolate chips

Directions: Preheat the oven to 325°F. Lightly coat a 9" x 13" pan with baking spray

In a large mixing bowl, cream together the butter, oil, sugar, vanilla, baking soda, baking powder, and salt. Beat in the eggs.

Stir in the yogurt alternately with the flour. Then add the cocoa mixing till smooth. Finally, fold in the zucchini and 1/2 cup chocolate chips. Spoon the batter into the prepared pan. Bake the cake for 35 – 40 minutes or until a cake tester inserted in the center comes out clean. Remove the cake from the oven and cool. To prepare the frosting, heat the heavy cream in a saucepan over medium heat until simmering. Remove from heat and pour over the chocolate chips. Wait 3 minutes then stir to combine. It may take a few minutes of stirring for the ganache to come together as it thickens as it cools. as when warm, but not super-hot, pour over cake and smooth with a spatula. Allow frosting to set for about 30 minutes before serving.

Marinated Zucchini Salad

You can make your own Italian dressing rather than buying the stuff in the bottle. I use a bottle when I'm in a pinch for time.

Ingredients:

4-5 small zucchini, cut into slices about 1/2 inch thick (or bite sized pieces)

1 can large pitted black olives, drained very well

1 jar marinated artichoke hearts, drained very well

1 red or green pepper chopped into bite-sized pieces

1 red onion chopped into bite-sized pieces

Crumbled Feta

Dressing Ingredients:

1 cup of Italian dressing

2 Tablespoons of fresh lemon juice (about one lemon)

1/4 cup grated Parmesan cheese

3 Tablespoons of chopped fresh basil

1 tsp. dried oregano

Directions: Cut zucchini into quarter slices or bite sized pieces. Steam zucchini until barely tender about 3 minutes, then submerge the steamed zucchini into water with ice cubes to stop the cooking. Drain well. While zucchini is cooking, open olives and artichoke hearts and dump into a colander to drain. (Draining the zucchini and olives well is essential or the finished salad will be watery.) Chop the red bell pepper and red onion into bite-sized pieces.

Combine zucchini, olives, artichoke hearts, red pepper and red onion in a container with a lid (or use a Ziploc bag.) Pour dressing over, just enough to cover veggies, and stir gently. (I usually only use part of the dressing to marinate the veggies and then stir in a little more dressing when I serve it.)

Marinate in refrigerator 4-8 hours. Just before serving stir in a little of the reserved dressing. Sprinkle the feta on top and gently mix in.

Fusilli Pasta with Roasted Tomatoes and "Hidden" Zucchini

CSA Member Sarah Hull

Ingredients:

6 plum tomatoes, halved lengthwise

2 teaspoons Olive Oil

Salt and ground black pepper to taste

1/2 cup Grated Parmesan Cheese, divided

1/4 cup chopped basil

1/2 pound Whole Wheat Fusilli (or whatever spiral pasta you can find)

2 zucchini or yellow squash, grated (we use 1 of each and grate it lengthwise on the box cheese grater)

2 Tablespoons lemon juice

Directions: Preheat oven to 400°F. Arrange tomatoes on a large parchment-lined sheet tray, cut-sides up. Drizzle with oil; season with salt and pepper. Scatter 2 tablespoons Parmesan and 2 tablespoons basil evenly over top. Roast until juicy and bubbling, about 20 minutes; set aside.

Meanwhile, bring a large pot of salted water to a boil. Add fusilli and cook until al dente, 10 to 12 minutes. Drain and transfer to a large bowl. Add zucchini, lemon juice, remaining 6 tablespoons Parmesan and 2 tablespoons basil. Toss to combine. Season to taste with salt and pepper.

Divide pasta onto four plates, top with tomatoes and serve.

Zucchini Cake

Chris Long

Here's another version of a zucchini desert

Ingredients:

½ cup of oil

½ cup of butter

1 ¾ cups of sugar

2 cups of zucchini, shredded

2 eggs

2 ½ cups of flour

½ cup of sour milk (add a 2 teaspoons of vinegar to the milk to "sour" it)

4 Tablespoons of Dutch pressed cocoa

1/2 teaspoons of baking soda

½ teaspoons of baking powder

½ teaspoon of cinnamon

1 teaspoon of vanilla

Directions: Preheat oven to 325 degrees. Mix wet ingredients together and in a separate bowl mix dry ingredients. Slowly combine and pour into a greased and floured 9X11 pan. Bake for 40-45 minutes.

Zucchini Boats

Cathy Helton

Ever have a GIGANTIC zucchini and the only thing you can make is bread? Try this instead! The amounts are relative because it just depends on how BIG your zucchini is!

Ingredients:

1 very large zucchini

Onion, diced

Tomato, diced

Green Peppers, diced

Olive Oil

Salt and Pepper

Garlic Salt

Directions: Slice the zucchini lengthwise and scoop out the seeds and some of the flesh to make a "boat." Fill the boat with tomatoes, onions and green peppers. Drizzle with olive oil and sprinkle with salt, pepper and garlic. Put the zucchini back together and wrap in foil. Grill for 30 minutes, turning after 15 minutes. Unwrap and enjoy!

Made in the USA
Middletown, DE
04 May 2015